A Taste of Home

And Other Short Stories

Suzanne Durant and
Dianne Weatherhead

A Taste of Home. Copyright © 2024 by Suzanne Durant and Dianne Weatherhead

All rights reserved.

No part of this publication may be reproduced, distributed, or transmitted in any form or by any means, including photocopying, recording, or other electronic or mechanical methods, without the prior written permission of the publisher, except as permitted by U.S. copyright law. For permission requests, contact Suzanne Durant or Dianne Weatherhead at **diandsuz@gmail.com**.

The story, all names, characters, and incidents portrayed in this production are fictitious. No identification with actual persons (living or deceased), places, buildings, and products is intended or should be inferred.

ISBN: 9798322584186 (paperback)

Book Cover by Eden Weekes

Contents

Dedication	V
A Taste of Home Dianne Weatherhead	1
Tea Times Suzanne Durant	11
Scent of Apartment 4D Suzanne Durant	20
A Weighty Case Dianne Weatherhead	28
Bajan Interrogation Suzanne Durant	34
A Rocky Road Dianne Weatherhead	47

Bajan Woman Suzanne Durant	56
One Cooked Goose Dianne Weatherhead	63
Our Little Secret Dianne Weatherhead	70
Her Perfect American Guy Suzanne Durant	76
Lost in Translation Dianne Weatherhead	90
Tech Me Home Suzanne Durant	97
Back in Time Dianne Weatherhead	107
High and Dry Clean Dianne Weatherhead	116
Supersized Supermodel Suzanne Durant	122
Glossary	131
Acknowledgements	135
Afterword	137
About the Authors	140

Dedicated to our Cawmere 6th Form WhatsApp group.
The best group of friends we could ever wish for.
Keep living well and laughing often.

A Taste of Home

Dianne Weatherhead

"Alaska?" three male voices rang out in unison. The domino that was about to be slammed onto the teak wood table hovered in mid-air, bringing the game to an immediate halt.

"Yeah, y'all hear me right. The boss sending me to Alaska for the next eight months," Donovan informed his buddies Cortez, nicknamed Perch, Eric, and James, as they lounged on the back patio of Donovan's suburban home. The early spring weather warranted an outdoor lime after the long Virginia winter months had them cooped up indoors.

"Man, your tail is really going to freeze up there," Perch laughed as he popped a savory fishcake into his mouth and washed it down with a gulp of mauby. Eric reached to turn down the old-school boombox that was blasting a reggae tune.

The men usually got together at least once every month or two just to chill out. Donovan and Perch had met back in primary school in Barbados and had maintained a close bond throughout their teenage years. As luck would have it, they both got accepted to the same college in Brooklyn, New York. Donovan pursued a degree in engineering, while Perch majored in computer science. After graduating, they each got a job offer in Virginia. A few months after moving, they met Eric and James, also Bajans, at a Caribbean-American Business Association fundraiser. Since then, they were a tight crew, each providing the others with what they all needed – a connection to their island home.

"Perch, our tails have been freezing right here in Virginia for the last eight years. And anyway, Alaska isn't cold all year. As my grandmother used to say, 'You went to school at the standpipe?' They have summer weather up there too, you know."

Cortez pursed his lips as he pondered Donovan's statement, demonstrating why he was re-christened "Perch" since primary school.

"Why you gotta push out your bottom lip so far when you thinking hard? You not frighten a bird take it for a perch and land on it?" one of his classmates had observed, making fun of Cortez in front of the entire class. From that day the moniker stuck, following him into adulthood.

"It isn't the cold that got me worried," Donovan said. "As much as I like to travel and try new foods, months without some good old Bajan cooking is a whole different thing," he lamented.

"Yeah man, you better brace yourself for some, shall we say, flavor-challenged food," said James. "I learned the hard way that a lot of people up here don't know a thing about lime-and-salting, much less seasoning chicken good, before cooking it. Some time ago, one of my co-workers invited me over for dinner after work. The man bring home a chicken, take it out of the plastic, ain't even wash it, sprinkle it with a little salt and pepper and stick it in the oven."

"And what you do?" Perch asked.

"What you think? I eat it," James answered with a hearty laugh. "After all, I couldn't insult the man. But just how you imagine a dog biscuit would taste is exactly how it tasted. That is why you always have to carry a little bottle of Bajan pepper sauce whenever you get invited to a meal."

The guys all chuckled and then shared their experiences of tasteless meals they had consumed over the years since living in the United States.

"When *Montego Pot* opened near my office, I was so happy to see a West Indian restaurant. The oxtail stew and rice and peas on point," said Eric.

The ringing of Perch's cell phone interrupted the banter. It was his aunt who lived nearby calling to say the pudding and souse she made was ready to be picked up.

A couple of hours later, after gourmandizing the pickled pork and steamed sweet potato, Donovan patted his stomach. "Now that is what you call a good plate of food."

"The only thing that coulda made that any better is a piece of roast breadfruit," said Eric, scraping the last remnants from his plate. "So you plan on traveling home before heading to Alaska?"

"Fuh sure. I've already booked a flight for next weekend. I plan to hit up Grafton's Village Shop for some bread-and-twos and Miss Hinds' Bakery for turnovers and leadpipes. Airport personnel will have to roll me out to the plane when it is time for me to leave." Donovan grinned.

"Awright fellas," Eric said, "leh we get back to the dominoes."

A loud "whapax" resounded as he slammed the domino onto the table.

If someone asked me to describe bliss, this would be it, Donovan thought, as his toes sank into the powdery white sand. He had arrived in Barbados the previous evening knowing it was his last trip for more months than he cared to think about. He walked a few feet farther along the beach and sat under a gnarled almond tree. Dappled rays of the late morning sun reached him between the branches as he appreciated the calming beauty of the view: small waves lapping onto the beach; an elderly couple enjoying the gentle massage of the crystal-clear water; anchored moses boats bobbing up and down, all against the backdrop of the cloudless cerulean sky. It never ceased to amaze him how people lived in this paradise and allowed years to pass without dipping a toe into the sea.

After enjoying a swim and the welcomed solitude, Donovan trekked back to his parents' home along a worn path through a pasture dotted with dunks trees. He smiled, recalling as a boy raiding the trees of their fruit, flying kites, and playing cricket on the patchy grass wicket.

When his parents arrived home from work, Donovan finally had an opportunity to chat with them about his extended stay in the northern state.

"So Don, how are you feeling about this Alaska business?" his father inquired.

"The truth is, it really could propel me up the ladder at work if everything goes as planned. It will be my first project as lead engineer, but I feel prepared."

"Well, I'm glad to hear that," his mother said. Sensing her son was not being totally open, she added, "But you seem a little subdued about the whole thing."

"Believe it or not, the hardest part will be missing the Bajan connection. You know how I like to hop on a plane and come home every two months or drive up to Brooklyn for the Bajan Day festivities."

"You're worrying too much about what you think you're going to be missing."

"Mum, you don't understand. Living overseas can be a difficult existence, especially with no family. It's a balancing act. You want to fit into a new culture, but you also want to maintain your own. You enjoy the differences, but you crave the familiarity of home. What keeps me going and grounded is hanging out with the guys and coming back to Bim as often as possible. You don't know how good it feels when you're in a store or on the train and hear a Bajan voice."

"You'll be alright." Grace placed a reassuring hand on her son's shoulder. "Things always have a way of working out."

"I know, Mum," he sighed softly, but quickly masked his uncertainty with feigned bravado, lowering the timbre in his voice. "Yeah, as man, I will be fine. But there's no place like home."

"So which part of Alaska will you be?"

"Mum, you're asking me that as if you know something about the place." Donovan laughed. His mother always needed every little piece of information. "And yes, I will send you the flight details and my address as soon as everything is arranged."

"Excuse me Mr. I-graduated-from-university." Grace placed her hands akimbo. "You don't know who, what or where I know."

"Sorry. Sorry, Mum," Donovan said. He never wanted his mother to feel he was disrespecting her or to come across as a know-it-all. "It is a small town called Ketchikan."

"Ketch-up can? What kind of name is that?"

"Ketch-i-kan," Donovan repeated slowly.

"Ketchikan... Ketchikan." His mum turned the name over in her mouth as if she was trying to taste it. "Hmmm... Ketchikan." Grace cocked her head to the side. "I think I've heard of that place before."

Donovan raised an eyebrow. "Anyway, I'm heading to Oistins to meet up with some fellas. You want me to bring back some grilled kingfish and macaroni pie for you and Dad?"

"Thanks son, but only from Miss Lashley's stall, please. You know I don't eat from everybody."

Grace turned to her husband who sat by the open front door trying to catch a slight breeze as he read the newspaper. "Luther, Eleanor home yet? Look across the road and see if her car is there. I want to find out if Albert Grandison still goes to her church."

"Yes, she's home. The old Toyota parked crooked as usual."

⇝⇝ ⇜⇜

The sun had barely risen when Eric dropped Donovan to the airport two weeks later.

"Thanks, my brother," Donovan said, retrieving his luggage from the trunk of the SUV.

"Anytime man," Eric replied. They gave each other a quick one-arm hug, slapping each other on the back. "I wish you the best. We will holla on the phone."

Donovan checked his itinerary as he waited to board the flight to Seattle, the first leg of his eleven-hour trip. In his two checked suitcases, packed among his clothes was a myriad of Bajan fare that included jars of aromatic homemade green seasoning, packets of sugar cakes, cassava pone, tamarind balls, Ovaltine and Tea Times biscuits, bottles of mauby syrup, Banks beers, and of course, pepper sauce, courtesy of James.

Donovan had a tedious three-hour layover before he boarded another aircraft to Ketchikan. Two hours later, the expansiveness of Alaska came into view. As far as the eye could see to the horizon, a green carpet of fir trees covered the land against a backdrop of majestic mountains with snow covered peaks. Donovan knew most of his days would be spent at the worksite, meeting with the various team members and ensuring the project stayed on track, but he was also looking forward to enjoying some of the sights and attractions of Alaska.

After collecting his luggage, he made his way out of the terminal, stopping short when he spotted his name written in large, black print on a piece of cardboard.

The travel coordinator never mentioned that a pickup had been arranged, he thought. Even more surprisingly, a tall, middle aged, black man held the sign. Before Donovan could identify himself, the hulking man made a beeline towards him.

"Hey, muh brudda, welcome to Ketchikan." He extended his hand to Donovan. There was no mistaking the distinctive Bajan cadence.

"Thank you." Donovan shook the stranger's hand. "How did you know...who...?" He was totally confused. The man smiled at Donovan's befuddled expression.

"I'm Vincent Grandison. My brother, Albert, asked me to meet you."

"I don't know any Albert Grandison," said Donovan, becoming even more perplexed.

"Well, apparently he knows your mother's neighbor, Eleanor Batson."

Donovan's brow furrowed, then everything fell into place. All he could do was shake his head at his mother's stealthy plan.

"I guess the saying is true. No matter where you go you could find a Bajan. So how did you end up here of all places?" Donovan asked.

"Man, that is a long, long, long story, but to break it down, I used to work on a cruise ship that sailed between California and here. About three years ago an opportunity opened up, so I took the chance and things are working out real nice."

"Well, it's good to know a fellow countryman nearby."

The ringing of the landline phone startled Grace just as she had settled into bed.

"That must be Don," she announced, reaching for the phone. "Hello."

"Hi Mum."

"Hi Don. You got to Alaska safely?"

"Yes, I'm good. I just called to let you know that Mr. Grandison picked me up at the airport. You're real slick though, Mum. I can't believe you pulled a fast one on me. The CIA ain't got nothing on you."

Grace chuckled. "You young people think we old folks are dotish, but we got some gas left in the tank."

"I'm not going to talk long. I know it's late there. It is only 6:30 p.m. here, so I'm trying to adjust to the time difference. We will talk again soon. Oh, Mr. Grandison invited me to his home for dinner tomorrow, and guess what? He'll be making cou-cou and saltfish."

"You see, son. I told you everything will be just fine."

Tea Times

Suzanne Durant

"So how long are you going to be in the US this time?" Hazel asked her best friend, Patricia, who was packing her suitcase for a flight scheduled to leave at six the next morning.

"I'll be there for about two weeks," Patricia said, wrapping a tee-shirt around a multi-pack of Tea Time biscuits.

Hazel surveyed Patricia's bed that was laden more so with a variety of Bajan consumables than clothes. There were sugar cakes, guava cheese, plantain chips, a 750-milliliter bottle of mauby syrup, a 750-milliliter bottle of pepper sauce, a two-pound block of cheddar cheese, two loaves of sweetbread, two 10-ounce bottles of Bajan seasoning and four Cadbury chocolates. The variety of biscuits was enough to fill a small store: Shirley biscuits, Ovaltine biscuits, Tea Time biscuits, Envita biscuits, Sodabix and Eclipse biscuits.

"You better be careful Customs don't hold you for traveling with all this stuff. You look like you going to open a shop."

Patricia laughed. "I have to keep my man well stocked until we see each other again, which won't be for another six months."

"You have more food than you have clothes, girl."

"I know. I don't need to take a lot of clothes since I'll be shopping, and by the time I offload this stuff on him, my suitcase will be empty. Don't forget that when he visits me, I have him traveling with all kinds of things too."

"That is true."

"Every time I travel with mauby for this man, though, the officials open my suitcase and leave a note in it. It's not the note that lets me know they've been in it but the way they have rummaged through my stuff and removed the cushioning from around the mauby. That tells me they've been in it."

"Pack it on the top of the suitcase instead of burying it in the middle. It's not like the bottle is glass. Once you secure the cap with tape and wrap the bottle in see-through plastic, you should be fine."

"Good idea. I'll do that with the pepper sauce too."

"At least when you two get married, you will be done with all this back and forth."

Patricia stupsed but playfully said, "Stop getting on us about being married. Noel and I are enjoying each other and the time we spend together when we can be face-to-face. We not looking at marriage yet."

"Well, you should be. How long has it been?"

"About three years now. But it doesn't feel that way. It just feels comfortable."

"Sooo . . . you planning to do this back-and-forth thing indefinitely?" Hazel held her chin between her thumb and index finger, eyeing Patricia curiously.

"Not indefinitely, but no one is rushing. We good."

"If my husband had taken this long to propose to me, especially if we lived in two different countries, I would not have been too happy about that."

"Well," Patricia said, tucking her last food item into the suitcase, "Noel and I are different. Now I need to chase you out of my house so I can get some sleep to get that early flight in the morning. You still picking me up at three thirty, right?"

"Of course," said Hazel. "You put the list of things I want in your handbag?"

"If I come back here without your things, you going make my life miserable. I am not about that."

"Am I that bad?"

"Worse. Now go. You need some sleep just like me," Patricia said, taking Hazel's arm and pulling her to the door.

"See you in about ten hours then."

With Hazel gone, Patricia finished packing and afterwards tidied up around her apartment. She brushed her teeth, put on her pajamas, and settled down in front of the television to watch a mystery movie before turning in, but the movie ended up watching her instead. She woke up in time to see the end of the movie where she learned who had committed the murder. Kicking herself internally, she sucked her teeth and went to bed. Just as her body relaxed to the point where it was welcoming sleep, the song *No One Inced the World* by Anita Baker belted out from her cell phone. That special ring tone could only be one person. Pushing her way out of the grogginess, she answered as cheerily as she could. "Hi baby."

"Hey you," came the rumble of Noel's voice over the line. "You sleeping already?"

"Just about to," Patricia said. "How you?"

"Since the last time we spoke, I'm fine. I had some baked chicken with potatoes and am now getting ready to sleep myself. But you know I had to hear your voice before I turned in."

"That's sweet. Looking forward to seeing you."

"Can't wait to see you too, honey. Sorry I wasn't able to get more time off from work so we could hang out during the week. But at least I have tomorrow off, and we have the weekend. And we can do stuff on evenings when I get in from work. There is so much I want to show you over here."

"And again, it's fine. I know how your job is. I love the fact that you get to move around from state to state too. I'm really looking forward to seeing Mississippi."

"I know," Noel said. "I really enjoyed my last assignment in Houston. But Meridian is nowhere near the size of Houston.

I may be in a small town but there's a lot to see. So you're all set for your trip?"

"Yup."

"You got my Tea Times?"

"Oh, so that is all you want?" Patricia could not help but giggle.

"But of course."

"So don't bother with the Shirleys, mauby, pepper sauce and all the other stuff then?" Patricia teased. "Just make sure I have the Tea Times?"

"You better leave my things in your suitcase. Just make sure you got both chocolate and vanilla Tea Times."

"Yes, sir. You will get your Tea Times. Now could I go get some sleep? You know I'm pushing off early too."

"Yes, sweets. Go get some rest and I will see you tomorrow. I love you."

"Love you too."

Patricia sat on the last leg of her journey to Mississippi anxious to touch down and see her boyfriend. As she made her way to the luggage carousel on arrival at the airport, she saw Noel sitting in the baggage claim area waiting for her. As soon as he spotted her, a smile spread across his face, and he quickly approached her and drew her into a warm embrace.

"You made it," he whispered into her ear. "I am so glad you're here. I've missed you, girl."

Patricia smiled up at Noel and planted a kiss on his lips. She knew she didn't need words to tell him that she felt the same.

They released each other and retrieved her two suitcases. It didn't take long for them to arrive as the flight had not been full. Noel grabbed them and they walked out into the parking lot to his truck chatting excitedly with each other.

"You hungry?" Noel asked as they pulled out of the airport parking lot.

"I could eat. I'm not a fan of airport food as you know, so I didn't eat much in Miami."

"Let's get you fed first then."

After eating, Noel stopped at a mall, telling her that he had to pick up his watch, which he had left to be repaired, from one of the stores.

"It's just the one store you going to for your watch?" Patricia asked.

"Yeah."

"How about you do that while I wander around this clothing store here. I see some things I like."

"You starting your shopping already? You not even waiting to settle in first?"

"Settle into what? We're here now. I might as well get started."

"We'll be back here in a couple days you know."

"I can shop some more then too." Patricia gave Noel a peck on his cheek and walked away smiling.

Just as I expected, Noel smirked as he walked to the jewelry store located at the other end of the mall, but it was not to pick up a watch.

Two hours and five shopping bags later they left the mall. Noel shook his head at his girlfriend as he drove to his place. It was 10:00 p.m. by the time they arrived, and they were both exhausted, so they took a bath and collapsed into bed.

The next morning, Noel and Patricia lazed around in bed enjoying each other's company. When they finally dragged themselves up around ten o'clock, Noel headed to the kitchen to make breakfast. After they had eaten, Noel washed the dishes while Patricia unpacked. The apartment was a studio with a counter dividing the kitchen from the small living area and the bed.

"Ok sir, I got all the stuff you wanted," Patricia told Noel who looked over at her with a grin.

"You are the sweetest," he said.

"Here's your mauby," Patricia said as she unpacked the items, "and your pepper sauce. Here's the Bajan seasoning. Oh, here's the cheese. You have to put that in the fridge right away. We should have done that last night."

"I'm coming." Noel took the cheese from her and put it in the fridge.

Patricia then meticulously unraveled each type of biscuit from the clothing they were wrapped in, announcing each brand and waving them at him.

"Here is your sweetbread... and your Ovaltine biscuits... Eclipse... Sodabix... Shirleys... Oh, here are your precious Tea Times..."

"The Tea Times," Noel exclaimed before Patricia could say another word. He ran out of the kitchen, retrieved a black velvet ring box from his bedside table and hurled himself across the bed to where Patricia was standing with the Tea Times still in her hand. Grabbing that same hand, he looked her directly in the eyes and said breathlessly, "Girl, I love you. Will you marry me?"

Patricia's mouth hung open for a few seconds as she tried to take in what had just happened. Finally, she said, "Noel, quit playing. You asking me to marry you just because I brought you Tea Times? I know you love the biscuits, but this is ridiculous." Patricia fell into a fit of giggles.

Looking down, Noel realized that Patricia was still holding onto two multipacks of Tea Times, vanilla and chocolate like he had requested, while his hands were locked around her wrists with the velvet box awkwardly jammed between her wrist and his hand. This was not at all how he intended his proposal to go, but seeing Patricia laughing so heartily made him laugh too, and after they both settled down, he slowly opened the box revealing a chocolate brown diamond engagement ring.

A year and a half later they were married, and Patricia never let him forget how he proposed to her over Tea Time biscuits.

Scent of Apartment 4D

Suzanne Durant

Leroy shifted his backpack from his left to his right shoulder as he climbed the stairs to his apartment on the fourth floor. He grumbled with each step about the inefficiency of the landlord; the elevator had been out of order for almost a week. After working a long, hard week from Tuesday night to Sunday afternoon, he was looking forward to his day off to relax and recharge for another grueling but satisfying week of work.

Leroy was a train conductor with the Metropolitan Transit Authority in New York City. He had migrated to the US only two years ago after his older brother, Troy, who had moved to the US shortly after leaving high school, had convinced him that he could make far more money there than back home in Barbados.

Leroy had done odd jobs here and there at home, but there hadn't been much going on for him in Barbados in terms of work, so with his brother's sponsorship, he moved to the Big Apple. His brother, who also worked with the MTA Transit system as a train driver, helped him get the job. Leroy lived for about a year with Troy and his wife, Cherille, so he could settle into his new life and job before moving into his own place. Troy had told his brother that he could stay as long as he liked, but Leroy really wanted to move out. It wasn't that he disliked living with Troy; he simply believed that as a married couple, Troy and Cherille needed their privacy.

He missed his island home but comforted himself with the fact that he had his brother who was just a twenty-minute train or bus ride away, and a job that not only paid very well, but was also enjoyable. Leroy liked meeting and engaging with the commuters he saw every day and took pride in making sure they were safe during their journeys.

As Leroy walked along the hallway to his apartment, he suddenly paused in front of Apartment 4D, which was just two doors away from his place.

Wait, he thought, sniffing the air. *That is sweetbread I smelling? Somebody in there baking sweetbread?* Leroy took a deep breath, allowing the spicy coconut scent to roll around in his nostrils and tease his taste buds.

Now, Leroy passed this door every day and had never gotten this delectable aroma before. He assumed either the tenants just started baking sweetbread or these were new tenants, maybe from Barbados or some other Caribbean island. He did not know the tenants because his work schedule did not give him much opportunity to see his neighbors, much less meet them. All he knew was this was the first time he wanted to stand in the hallway, typically invaded by the unpleasant moldy odor of a carpet that desperately needed cleaning, and inhale the sugary sweetness wafting around him.

The last time the smell of sweetbread hit him so forcefully was before he left Barbados to move to the US. His mother, a master at baking, made sweetbread twice a month to sell and give away, and she always had two hefty loaves for Leroy. Pavlov's dogs let loose in Leroy's mouth, and he had to swallow hard to prevent himself from dribbling. Reluctantly, he continued to his apartment but not before taking one last, lingering sniff before entering his sanctuary and consoling himself with the belief that the sweetbread had to be a one-off thing.

The following Sunday as Leroy returned home, the tantalizing smell hit him again.

"Man, no man," Leroy said out loud.

He stood outside of 4D, tempted to knock, but he knew how funny New Yorkers were about people they did not know. This was not Barbados. In his little village back home, everyone knew each other, and you could go to anyone's house and be welcomed with a drink or something to eat. Leroy stood there salivating and had to force himself to move away from the door.

Leroy rarely ran into his brother at work because they were on two different train lines, so at least twice a month when he and his brother had the same day off, Leroy visited Troy at his home. On his next visit, he shared his experience with the scent of the sweetbread from Apartment 4D.

"You sure you not just imagining things?" his brother chuckled.

"My man, I know what sweetbread smell like. How you mean if I imagining things?" Leroy said and released a big stupse.

"You just lef home you know, so you might still be feeling a little homesick. Your mind might be playing tricks on you."

"My mind working just fine. I know what I smelling. It smelling just like Mum sweetbread," Leroy insisted, determined not to let his brother make him feel like he was hallucinating.

"If you so sure bout it, why you don't go and knock on the door and ask for some," Troy suggested with a serious face at first, and then burst out laughing.

"Stop teasing your brother, Troy," Cherille piped in. "If the man say he smelling sweetbread, then that is what he smelling."

"This isn't Barbados. I ain't going knocking on no stranger door. Next thing I waking up in the hospital. I ain't that hard up for lil sweetbread. When I go back home in a couple years, I will get my sweetbread from Mum, or if anyone we know coming up, we could get them bring it up," Leroy affirmed.

"If you change your mind and decide to take a chance with the neighbor, get some for me, hear," Troy said, this time howling with laughter.

"You right to make mock sport at me," Leroy said. "But if the neighbor offer me any, I going think bout you as I eat every crumb."

※

Two weeks later, Leroy called Troy. "Boy, you won't believe this!"

"What happen?"

"You home tomorrow?"

"Yeah. You swinging by?"

"Once you and Cherille don't have any plans."

"Come through bro," Troy said.

Monday afternoon, Leroy arrived at Troy's apartment and fixed himself a brandy before reclining on the two-seater couch. He dropped his backpack next to the chair.

"What happen to you, bro? You look offset," Troy said, watching him closely.

"Check this. I went to the neighbor yesterday after work. I just couldn't take the smell no more. I had to get piece of that sweetbread," Leroy confessed after taking a sip of his drink.

Troy sniggered and took a seat opposite his brother. "You couldn't help yourself, nuh? So yuh get piece of sweetbread?"

"Well first off, it is two young Bajan girls living there. They just move in a month ago. They at university."

"Oh man. Bajans? That is great. Which one is the baker?"

"That is the thing. After introducing myself, I tell them bout the mouthwatering smell of sweetbread I get every Sunday from their apartment when I get home from work and asked if they would mind sharing, seeing as we are practically family, being from Barbados and all." Leroy took another sip of his drink.

Troy watched his brother for a few seconds before saying, "So, where my piece of sweetbread?"

Leroy looked at Troy and chuckled. "If I don't laugh, I going cry. In fact, I almost cry when they brought me the sweetbread."

"Well it is my turn to ask you to share, seeing as we from Barbados and all," Troy teased.

Leroy looked at his brother and shook his head. He drained his glass before turning to his backpack. After slowly unzipping it, he reached inside and pulled out a brown paper bag. Troy watched in anticipation as Leroy put his hand in the bag and pulled out an oblong brown box the size of a small tissue box.

"These girls special enough. They give you a slice of sweetbread in such a fancy looking box. They could have just wrapped it up in wax paper or something," Troy said, but by this time his mouth had started to water in anticipation of the treat. It looked like his brother had really pulled it off and gotten a piece of the precious baked goods after all.

Leroy said nothing. He slowly opened the box while eyeing Troy. When he removed the cover, Troy craned his neck, positioning his nose to catch the first whiff of coconut, vanilla and nutmeg. But lo and behold, nestled cozily in the box was a three-inch, beige, cylindrical candle encased in a glass container. Leroy removed the candle from the box and put it on the glass-top coffee table between them. He pulled a box of matches from his pocket and lit the wick. All the while, Troy watched his brother as if he were crazy. Ten seconds later, the sweet, coconut, spicy aroma of sweetbread wrapped itself around Troy's apartment.

"A candle?" Troy said, his face contorted into a look of confusion and his mouth open.

"Hear this," Leroy began. "These girls wanted a piece of home, since they going be up here about three years studying. So they went to Pelican Village to this store that does sell candles with Bajan scents like the beach, the market, rum and sugar cane. That is where they find this sweetbread candle. You could believe that?"

By this time, Troy was rolling around on the ground holding his belly and laughing. When he cooled down enough to look at Leroy, he saw his brother making a call.

"Wait, who you calling?" he asked.

"Mummy!" Leroy said. "I been tortured by that candle for a whole month. Time to get the real thing now. As for you,

you might as well stop laughing at me because as I was opening the damn box you looked like you was ready to grab what was inside before I get a chance to open it properly. Hello Mummy," Leroy said, turning his attention from his brother to his mother.

"Tell Mummy send some sweetbread for me too...hold the wax," Troy whispered loudly before melting into more laughter.

A Weighty Case

Dianne Weatherhead

The buzzing vibration of her cell phone roused Keisha awake. She fumbled for the device on her nightstand. Peering through bleary eyes at the brightly illuminated screen, her brain registered the time - 6:22 a.m.

"Who could be calling me so early on a Saturday morning?" she garbled to no one. She didn't recognize the number displayed, but decided to answer anyway just in case it was an urgent matter.

"Hello?" Keisha mumbled hoarsely.

"Hi Keisha!" An exuberant voice greeted her. "Girl, how you?"

"Who is this?"

"This is Faronda Ifill."

"Faronda Ifill? Who?" Keisha flipped through her mental rolodex but failed to recall the name.

"What do you mean, 'who?'" the caller asked, sounding offended. "That used to work at Varhinge with you."

The lingering vestiges of sleep slipped away, clearing Keisha's memory. She hadn't seen or heard from her ex-coworker in almost three years. The two had worked at an electronics distribution center just outside of the downtown Philadelphia, Pennsylvania area. Well, Keisha worked. Faronda did as little as possible, spending most of her shift flitting from workstation to workstation gossiping instead of processing the customers' orders.

Unfortunately for Keisha, when Faronda discovered that they were both of Barbadian descent, Faronda became as annoying as a mosquito, interrupting Keisha daily with, "Hi Bajan sis" and chatting about scandals that had taken place on the island. Since Keisha was American-born and had only spent a few summers in Barbados as a child with her grandparents, she had no interest in the gossip, and tried her utmost to avoid the garrulous woman. After four months of employment, their manager refused to tolerate Faronda's idleness, and he terminated her.

"So why are you calling me, and how did you get my number?"

"I got it from Suzy Seaford who works with you. I ran into her yesterday, and I asked her how you were doing, and she mentioned that you were traveling to Barbados in a couple days."

"And?"

"And I was wondering if you could do me a favor and take a couple items down there for me?"

Keisha held the phone away from her ear and looked at it as if it were sprouting horns. *I can't be hearing right. This has to be a prank call.*

"You're seriously calling me at this hour, after all this time, to ask me for a favor?"

"I know it's early, but I just got home from working my shift and I'm about to go to sleep myself, too, so I wanted to call you as soon as possible," Faronda replied unabashedly. "My sister is pregnant and craving nuts, so I want to send two cans of cashews for her. You know how expensive things are down there. So, you could take them for me?"

Keisha shocked herself by agreeing to the request. Although the single suitcase she planned to take was already bulging with items for her own family, she figured she could find a little space for two small tins.

"Thanks so much. I can pass by tomorrow morning around eleven-ish to drop them off."

"Okay, I will text you my address. I may not be at home, but my nephew will be here."

Ending the call, Keisha shook her head, marveling at the audacity of some people. She snuggled back under the sheets and drifted off to sleep again.

The following day, after attending a worship service and running a few errands, Keisha returned home. The living room was cluttered with her opened suitcase and a few odds and ends yet to be packed. She noticed a gray duffle bag on the table in the adjacent dining room and was pleasantly surprised her teenage nephew had organized his carry-on luggage already since he usually did everything at the last minute.

"Jeff!" she shouted up the stairs. "Did the lady come by with the package?"

"Yes Auntie," he replied.

"Where did you put it?"

"It's in the dining room."

Keisha glanced over her shoulder, scanning the area. "I only see your duffle bag on the table."

"That isn't my bag. That's what the lady brought."

Faronda couldn't find a smaller bag? Keisha thought, as she walked back to the dining room and unzipped the satchel.

"What is all of this?" Keisha hollered. Her eyes bulged and her jaw slackened when she saw the contents: two tins of cashews the size of breadfruits and just as heavy, a gigantic jar of cocoa butter that could liberally cover an elephant's entire body, and a huge plastic bottle of manuka honey hair moisturizer that rivaled a two-liter soda bottle. A folded piece of paper lay on the bottom of the bag. Scrawled on it was a name, an address, and a phone number.

Blue vex and muttering repeatedly, "She can't be serious," Keisha grabbed her cell phone from her handbag. She had silenced it when she had settled into a pew before the morning church service started and had neglected to check it before heading home. She now saw a text from Faronda:

> "Hey. Just left ur house. Sending a couple other items for my sister. Cream to help with her stretch marks and hair conditioner. Pregnancy causing her hair breakage. If you have to pay for overweight at airport let her know. When you drop off things she will reimburse you. Thanks. Enjoy ur trip."

"Pay for overweight? When I drop off things?" Keisha barked. She tossed the hulking items back into the bag, roughly hauled it to the hallway closet and slammed the door shut. "If she thinks I'm going somewhere with those things, she nuttier than them cashews."

Still fuming, Keisha started to call her girlfriend to vent about Faronda's brazenness, only to realize there was a second text she had missed.

> "BTW, bring back some Bajan cheese for me plz. The extra-large 2kg/4 ½ lb. block. Thanks."

"Talk about gall! She might as well ask me to bring back a cement brick." Keisha rolled her eyes. "She could hold she breath and wait fuh it!"

Bajan Interrogation

Suzanne Durant

July 20th was fast approaching, and Fiona was excited. Her grandmother was coming to visit her and her mother, Marlene, in New York for four weeks. In the time leading up to the arrival, Fiona had gone out of her way to make sure her granny's room was neat and tidy, just the way she knew she would like it, and she had badgered her mother to make sure and get all the things from the Caribbean grocery that she knew her granny would like. At first, Marlene had told her that there was no need to make such a fuss, but she relaxed, reminding herself that Fiona had not seen her granny in the flesh for over three years.

"Look Mummy. There she is." Fiona pointed her finger in the direction of her slow-moving granny. Fiona raced over to the elderly lady and wrapped her in a warm hug. Then she relieved her of her suitcase, and holding her by her hand, led her over to her mother. The two women lovingly embraced before they all headed to the parking lot.

"It's so good to see you, Granny," Fiona gushed for about the twentieth time on the drive home.

"It real good to see you too, chile. Look how grown up you are," Granny said smiling broadly.

"Well, you know Ma, you always say they don't stay small," Marlene said.

They continued chatting on the twenty-five minute journey home about the weather and goings-on in Barbados and New York.

When they finally arrived home, Fiona took the suitcase upstairs to Granny's room. She returned downstairs to the kitchen, where her mother was preparing a cup of tea for her grandmother. Just as she was about to start throwing questions at her granny, Marlene stopped her.

"It's late, Fiona. Let Granny get some rest. That flight took a lot out of her, you know."

"The flight was good," Granny said, "but uh feel tired in trute."

"Plus, you have work tomorrow," Marlene reminded her daughter.

Glancing at the clock, Fiona saw that it was just after 10:30 p.m. As it was summer, darkness did not descend on New York until 9:00 p.m. and as long as Fiona had been living there, the seasonal change still threw her off. She gave her granny a squeeze, wished her a good night and headed off to bed.

Fiona could not contain her excitement. She had been raised by her granny until she was eleven. Marlene had met an American man in Barbados when Fiona was just six years old, and after dating long distance for two years, had gotten married to him in Barbados before migrating to the US. Marlene wanted to take Fiona with her, but her mother convinced her to let Fiona stay and complete her primary school education. With visits between Barbados and the United States by both mother and daughter, the pair settled into the routine without any problems.

After completing the Common Entrance examination and learning she had passed for Christ Church Foundation School, Fiona had made her bitter-sweet departure from Barbados to New York to be with her mother and stepfather. She was sorry she did not get to attend Foundation, and she missed her grandmother terribly, but quickly settled into her life in the US.

She enrolled in middle school before moving on to high school where she did very well in both instances. She then applied to university to study finance. In her third year, she met Kristopher, also a Bajan, who had migrated to the US with his parents when he was seven years old. She and Kristopher were now out of college and working as professionals in their fields, he as a business analyst and she as a personal banker.

"Hi baby," she cooed into the phone from under the cover of her blanket. She regularly spoke to her boyfriend before turning in.

"Hey sugar. Did your grandmother arrive okay?"

"Yes. She's downstairs having her bay leaf tea. She's really tired so she'll be heading to bed soon."

"You're in bed but you don't sound tired."

"It's the excitement of seeing my granny. I haven't seen her in person for three years now and I have really missed her. FaceTime is fine but it's not the same. Plus, it's her first time here."

"I got you. So when do I meet her?"

"Most likely this weekend, like Saturday. I'm not sure if she will want to stay in and rest up a bit more. The trip has taken a lot out of her."

"That's no problem. I know how it is. Saturday then. What time you want me to come by?"

"Come and have dinner with us. Around six?"

"I'll be there."

The following day, Fiona hurried home from work to spend some time with her granny. After dinner, the two settled into the living room to catch up with each other's lives. Granny filled her in on what was happening on the television shows *The Bold and The Beautiful* and *Days of our Lives*.

"Honestly, Granny, the way you talk, you would think those people were real," Fiona said, giggling.

"Young lady, don't fool yuh foot. They might be TV shows, but the things going on in them does happen in real life," Granny said authoritatively, peering over her half-moon reading glasses at Fiona.

"I have some news for you that is not on TV, Granny," Fiona said, changing the subject.

"You got a promotion? Wait, I hope you not pregnant?"

"Not yet to the promotion and Granny, how you could ask me if I pregnant? You know I'm not," Fiona said.

"Don't be so shocked about the pregnancy question. You old enough for a bun to be in that oven. You don't have a man?"

"I have a boyfriend, Granny," Fiona said blushing.

"He ain't a man? Who is this boyfriend you got now?"

"We met at university. We been together for about three years now."

"All the time that we talked, you sounded real busy. You got time for boyfriend?"

"Yes, my job is busy but I really love Kris. You going meet him tomorrow evening. He's coming over for dinner."

"This boy white? He is American?"

"No, Granny. He is black and he is a Bajan."

"I had to ask because from what I seeing on TV, they got a lot of mix couples bout this place. I ain't got no problem with you bringing home a white boy. He would just have to appreciate the Bajan in you, you understand me?"

"I understand, Granny," Fiona smirked. "Kris is Bajan. He moved here when he was young, primary school age."

"Bajans too love to move up here. Uh mean tings cheap, but I don't see the big attraction to this city. I been here only one night so far but the sirens and noise on the streets don't let you get nuh rest atall. How you all does manage?"

"We manage very well," came Marlene's voice from the doorway. She walked into the living room and sat opposite her mother.

"I hope you soon planning to move out of this noisy area to some place quieter. I really couldn't live here."

"At some point in time, Ma. It benefits all of us right now to be living in the heart of Brooklyn. Besides, we like it here."

"Back to this boy Kris," Granny said, turning her attention back to Fiona. "You really know this boy?"

"Of course I know him. He comes by the house all the time."

"So why he not here now?"

"I told you, Granny, he will be here for dinner tomorrow. You will get to meet him then."

"And Ma," Marlene gave a knowing look to her mother, "do not interrogate the poor young man, you hear?"

"Me? Interrogate?" Granny rocked her body left then right and looked reproachfully at her daughter over her glasses. "I going just chat with the boy. What wrong with you?" She rolled her eyes and stupsed.

Fiona looked from her mother to her grandmother, clueless as to why her mother would issue such a warning.

"Hi babe," Kristopher said, planting a kiss on Fiona's lips as she greeted him at the door. He had arrived at 6:00 p.m. sharp and was looking forward to seeing Fiona and spending time with her family. He liked her mother and stepfather but was a tiny bit nervous about meeting her grandmother.

Fiona escorted him into the living room, and he took a seat while she went to get her granny. Kristopher stood up when they entered the living room, and after the introductions, he extended his hand, which she took and firmly shook. Kristopher's first impression of Granny was that she looked like a sweet old lady. She was petite at five feet, and, not plump, but stoutly built. She had a gentle looking face with eyes bright like Fiona's. Kristopher immediately felt comfortable with her.

Fiona helped Granny into an armchair while she sat close to Kristopher on the couch. Suddenly, Granny rose from her seat, shuffled over to the couch, and stood between Fiona and Kristopher. Before the young people could properly process what was happening, Granny shifted her ample behind from side to side and eased down between Fiona and Kristopher, forcing them to make room for her. Fiona almost fell off the couch as she adjusted her position.

"Aaahhh," Granny said, sounding like a tire releasing air as she sank onto the couch and looked from Fiona to Kristopher, smiling. "Much better."

"Okay." Kristopher stretched the word out, feeling a mixture of confusion and embarrassment while glancing over at Fiona. He didn't even realize he had spoken out loud.

Fiona, meanwhile, looked at her granny questionably and merely shrugged at Kristopher.

"Uh . . . how was your flight from Barbados?" Kristopher said, trying to regroup. He felt like getting up and sitting in another seat but did not want to appear rude.

"It was good. Uh here, right?" Granny said, turning her head and carefully eyeing Kristopher.

Even though Fiona had scooted over on the couch to make room for Granny, Granny had not shifted herself away from Kristopher, so their faces were mere inches apart. The young man felt extremely uncomfortable being so close to Fiona's grandmother, but again he was determined to make the best of it. He did not want to come over as disinterested in the elderly woman.

"Do you have any special plans for this trip? Anywhere in particular you want to go?"

"This is my first time here, so I leaving it up to Fiona and Marlene," said Granny, peering over her spectacles and eyeing him without blinking.

.

"I'm taking a few days off next week so I can join you and Mummy. Maybe you can join us next weekend, Kris, when we take Granny sightseeing."

"Speaking of sightseeing," Granny said before Kristopher could open his mouth to respond. "When last you were in Barbados?"

"I have not been back for a while, maybe about five years or so," he said.

"What is your last name again?" Granny asked, knowing full well she had not asked for it in the first place.

"Brathwaite."

"Brathwaite," Granny said, rolling the name around in her mouth. "What part of Barbados you from?"

"Greenhill. We used to live in Greenhill."

"I knew some Brathwaites in Greenhill. Who you living here with?"

"Gran..." Fiona began.

"I just asking the boy a few questions. Something wrong with that?"

"It's alright Fi," Kristopher jumped in. "I live with both my parents. About 20 minutes away from here too."

"Oh, so your parents still together. They married?"

Kristopher chuckled. "Yes."

"What was your mother's name before marriage?'

"Granny," Fiona interrupted, alarmed with her granny's behavior. She could not remember her grandmother being like this with anyone. "Are you a reporter or working for the FBI or something?"

"Listen," Granny said, "I need to understand this young man's background. He could be your cousin."

"Kris is not my cousin, Granny," Fiona said laughing.

"How you know?" Granny asked sharply. "There are cases where people married their cousins and did not even know it was their cousin."

Fiona stopped laughing when she saw granny's serious expression. She looked over at Kristopher who had a puzzled look on his face.

"Ahhh . . . I going and help mummy and come back," Fiona said, getting up from the couch to run into the kitchen but not before noticing the urgent look in Kristopher's eyes that were begging her to stay.

When she disappeared, Granny turned back to Kristopher who gave her a nervous smile.

"So you were telling me your mother's name."

"Uh . . . ah . . . my mother's name used to be Spooner."

"I know some Spooners not too far out in Eden Lodge. That is where your mother used to live?"

"I think so,"

"Your father lived in Greenhill all his life?"

"No. They only moved there after he and my mother got married." By now, Kristopher felt as if Granny had an imaginary gun pointed at him and if he didn't answer her questions, she would let him have it. This "sweet, old lady" was nobody to play with.

"Your mother's name was Janet Spooner by any chance?"

"Uh, no. It was Margaret Spooner, now Margaret Brathwaite."

"And your father, where he grow up Barbados?"

"My father's side of the family is from St. George."

"Wait, Fiona got family in St. George."

"Really? Wow!" was all Kristopher could think to say as he felt sweat trickling down the nape of his neck.

"Yes. My brother lived there for a while too. What your father name?"

"Ma," Marlene, trailed by Fiona, burst into the room carrying a small glass of brown liquid, which she thrust into Granny's hand. "Why are you out here interrogating this boy so? He is not related to us. He and Fiona are fine."

Granny put the glass to her lips and took a long sip before responding. "You never can tell. You asked him already who his parents are? His mother is Margaret." Granny turned her attention back to Kristopher. "You didn't tell me your father's name."

Fiona quickly spoke up. "His father's name is Harry Brathwaite."

"Hm," Granny said, and took another sip. "The food ready, Marlene?"

"Yes, Ma, the food ready. Let's go," Marlene said, taking her mother by the arm and helping her out of the chair.

"You look at that little fella good, though?" Granny asked as she walked next to her daughter. "You don't find he features Ophneal that live out by me? Come to think of it, he look a lot like your cousin Seymour. He got them same black eyes and them bat ears."

"Mummy, come along before the food gets cold," Marlene said, completely ignoring her comment about Kristopher.

Fiona went and stood next to her boyfriend and held onto his arm as they followed the others.

"Your grandmother can ask some questions, girl," Kristopher whispered.

"I didn't see all that coming," Fiona said apologetically.

"What's that drink your mother gave her? It looked like a shot of something."

"Granny likes a little Extra Old Rum before dinner, and later you will see her drinking gin and tonic."

"Oh, Granny like drinks," Kristopher said, laughing.

"You better have some too," Fiona advised.

"Oh? Why?"

"My mother tell me Granny not done with you yet. This is intermission."

"Whaaat? I really feel like I being interrogated by the Bajan CIA."

"From what my mother told me in the kitchen, formal intelligence services ain't got nothing on an interrogation from a Bajan granny."

A Rocky Road

Dianne Weatherhead

Latrice reached for her favorite rock in her ever-growing collection: a smooth, black obsidian nugget. She kept it on the tiny bedside table in her college dorm. The glassy rock, about the size of a walnut, had a strange way of calming her nervousness when she rubbed it between her thumb and index finger. A light sheen of sweat settled across her forehead making her skin gleam. She was more anxious than an accused awaiting a jury's verdict as she prepared to make her weekly Sunday call to her father.

"Please, please, please let the answering machine pickup," Latrice prayed, but she already knew that was unlikely. She wasn't sure how to break the news to her father that she had changed her course of study. Worse still, how would she tell him the new academic path she had chosen?

"Hello, Trice!" Sylvan Hall eagerly answered his old, corded phone. He refused to get a cell phone no matter how hard Latrice tried to persuade him. He also refused to call her by her given name. She was always Trice.

A year had passed since she left her island home Barbados to attend university in America to study business and accounting. It was the day after celebrating her nineteenth birthday when she had ripped open the envelope containing the letter informing her that she had been awarded a full academic scholarship. She could hardly wait to tell her father, and he in turn couldn't wait to share the news with any and every one he encountered.

Sylvan, a twelve-year veteran of the Barbados Transport Board, the main public bus service on the island, drove the Bridgetown to Bathsheba route. Passengers marveled at how this twig of a man expertly maneuvered the large vehicle along the tight bends of the narrow country roads. When a familiar passenger boarded the vehicle and greeted him, he responded with proud excitement, "My daughter going to university in America to study business."

Although Latrice had earned an academic scholarship, Sylvan had to get a loan from his credit union to cover her basic living expenses. The strain of finding odd jobs to make the monthly payments, however, was worth the effort.

"Hi Daddy. How are you?" Latrice tried to sound as cheery as possible, but she was too anxious to mask the stilted cadence in her voice.

"I'm good Trice," he answered. "Everything alright?"

"Umm, yes." Latrice chewed her bottom lip and rubbed the stone between her fingers even faster as a bead of perspiration rolled down her high cheek bone. "Daddy," she paused, then blurted out her confession. "I decided to change my degree to something else."

Sylvan sat forward in his old caned-back mahogany chair, yanking the twisted phone cord, almost pulling the base off the kitchen counter where it sat.

"What you mean you changing your degree? I am not understanding you clearly." Deep furrows formed in Sylvan's already creased forehead. "To what?"

"Well, remember I told you I took some science classes last semester and did really well?"

"Yes, I remember. So you want to study medicine or something like that?" Sylvan asked as he relaxed back into the chair.

"Not exactly, Daddy. I want to study geology."

"Geology?" Sylvan asked. "I never heard bout that. What exactly is geology?"

Latrice took a deep breath. "It's learning about the earth's structure. Like how it was formed and the different types of rocks..."

Sylvan bolted up from the chair, interrupting Latrice. "Rocks? You and dese rocks! Now you want to learn bout rocks? Nah, nah, I can't be hearing you right!"

"Daddy, it's not just about rocks. It's more than that. Just hear me out," she pleaded.

"You got to be mekking sport. You think I send you up there to be looking at rock stones? I send you to get a good education to come back here and get a good job in a bank or one of them big insurance companies, and you telling me about studying rocks. Who you think bout here going hire you to look at rocks?" Sylvan stupsed long and hard.

Hearing her son's raised voice from her bedroom, his mother, Irene, hustled as quickly as her arthritic knees would allow to the kitchen. "Sylvan? What going on out here that you keeping all dis noise?" she asked, perplexed.

Sylvan thrust the phone at her. "Here, you talk to your granddaughter because she like she lost she mind." He stormed to the front door, roughly slid on a pair of slippers and left the house.

Irene caught the receiver before it hit the floor. "Latrice, what you say to your father?"

"Gran, I'm sorry that I upset Daddy. I know he wants the best for me, but I don't see myself crunching numbers for a living." Latrice choked back a sob. She went on to share the decision she had made.

"Sweetheart, I don't know what a geologist is, but if that is what you want to do, follow your heart and pray about it." Irene sighed as she looked out the window at Sylvan pacing in the front yard of the small bungalow. "You know he just want you to get a good job, but he will get over this eventually."

"I hope so, Gran. Tell Daddy I will talk to him next Sunday."

When she called the next week, her father was not at home. Nor was he there the following three Sundays. With each call, her heart sank deeper and deeper. Was it worth it to follow her passion at the risk of jeopardizing her relationship with her only parent? She had lost her mother three years earlier when she fell into a diabetic coma and the doctors had been unable to revive her. Irene continued to be as supportive as she could be of her only granddaughter.

As a child growing up in Barbados, Latrice loved collecting rocks. Her family and friends couldn't understand why she was so fascinated with the odd-shaped pieces of coral she found on the beach or the limestone fragments with tiny shells embedded in them. Her first tour of Harrison's Cave rendered her virtually speechless as the crystalline stalagmites and stalactites mesmerized her. Year after year, the only birthday gift she begged for was a visit to the subterranean natural attraction. The year she turned thirteen, the cave was closed for renovation, and she was heart-broken. When her cousin brought her a piece of volcanic rock from his trip to neighboring St. Vincent, her high-pitched squeal almost deafened him. Latrice spent hours online researching famous rock formations like Ayers Rock in Australia and the Grand Canyon in America. "One day I'm going there," she promised herself.

Of course, no one, especially her father, ever fathomed that Latrice's hobby would ever be more than just that — a hobby. He had high hopes for her, and they certainly didn't involve rocks.

As the years passed, Latrice continued to call her father, but his disappointment in her decision never waned. However, she didn't harbor any resentment towards him. Her love for her father was just as strong as it had always been.

Latrice took classes during the summer vacations to ensure she graduated within the standard four years of study for an undergraduate degree. It was challenging academically and financially, but she managed to successfully complete the geology program, graduating with honors. Her resolve, however, had prevented her from taking trips back to Barbados to see her family, but she was finally returning home.

"What I gine tell people when they ask me what Trice doing now that she finished up at university?" Sylvan bemoaned to his mother as they ate their Sunday lunch. "How after getting a degree, she doing *field work* out in the hot sun all day? What foolishness is that?"

"Sylvan, the chile say she got a good job working for a good company. As long as she doing an honest day's work that is all that matters. You should just be glad that your daughter come back home."

"But you know if malicious Audrina up the road ever get wind that Trice don't have an office job the whole of Barbados will know," Sylvan grumbled, as he cleared the empty plates from the table. "Since her son get that job at the Central Bank, she always parading up and down the neighborhood, acting like she is the one that does mek the sun rise every morning. And mind you, he is only the security guard."

Later that afternoon, Latrice arrived at her father's house. It seemed smaller than she remembered, but the narrow front yard and verandah were still pristinely maintained. She wiped her sweaty palms along her denim-clad thighs and exited the taxi.

Latrice threw her arms around her father as he met her at the wrought-iron gate. Sylvan couldn't hide his joy at seeing his daughter as he held her tightly. Irene, too, eagerly embraced Latrice.

"Let me get a good look at you." Irene guided her granddaughter to twirl. "You put on some weight, girl. You looking rosy enough," she said, beaming with delight.

They all settled into the living room. Latrice told stories of her adventures in America, including her dream trip to the Grand Canyon, while Sylvan and Irene shared the local gossip.

"So Daddy, you heard about the Labyrinth Environmental Project that will be starting soon? I know it has been in the news recently."

"You mean the one that got something to do with a new cave system they discover, and how it could cause sinkholes under people houses?"

"Yes, that is exactly the problem. Well, I will be part of the team," Latrice said, smiling proudly.

"So what *exactly* will you be doing?" Sylvan asked hesitantly.

Latrice ventured cautiously into her response. "During phase one, I'll be surveying the caves, looking at the natural water-drainage patterns, taking rock samples and..." She gently raised her hand to stop her father from interrupting her. "Yes, Daddy I'll be doing field research, and that's what I enjoy doing. You may see it as dirty work, but I love that part of the job."

"It sounds like it could be dangerous though," said her grandmother.

"I'll be very careful Gran," Latrice assured her. "Every precaution is taken whenever we go exploring. During phase two, I'll be spending most of my time analyzing data, creating reports and making recommendations. Y'all know the new office building where Island Fresh Supermarket used to be?"

"Yes, that is a real fancy building. I hear it cost nuff money and got state-of-the art technology. Some foreign people own it," Sylvan replied.

"Well, that is where the company I'll be working for is located. And yes Daddy, I *will have* an office."

"Fuh real?" Sylvan beamed. "My girl going be working in style then?"

Latrice grinned at the relief and pride that lit up her father's face. Suddenly, he leapt from his chair, hurriedly put on his slippers and raced out the door.

"Sylvan, where you going in such a hurry?" Irene shouted before he reached the gate.

"Down by Audrina," he answered, grinning smugly from ear to ear.

Bajan Woman

Suzanne Durant

Peter loosened his tie as he took his usual seat at Culpepper Bar. He'd had a long hard day at work crunching numbers and needed a drink to relax before heading home.

"The usual, Pete?" Nick the bartender asked as he wiped the counter.

"No beer tonight, Nick. Need something a little stronger this time. Give me a vodka and orange juice, heavy on the vodka."

"You had a rough one?"

"When you see me in here at this kind of time, yes."

"Coming up."

Peter glanced around the small bar as he waited for Nick to bring his drink. He noticed a chubby guy with a bald head sitting at a table a few yards away eating French fries and drinking a beer. And he looked awfully familiar. *Wait a minute,* he thought. *That can't be.* He had not seen this man since secondary school ten years ago. Nick brought Peter's drink, and after Peter thanked him, he got up and walked over to the man.

"Winston? Winston Greene?" he asked.

The man looked up. Surprise, followed by a broad smile, erupted on his face.

"Wait, Peter Dowell?" Winston said and stood up.

The two men shook hands and hugged shoulder to shoulder, and Winston invited Peter to have a seat at his table.

"Man, how long has it been, man?" Winston asked.

"Too many years, bro. Too many years. What you been up to?"

"When I left school, I moved to New York to live with my father. I went straight to university and then got a job in marketing at a small firm. What about you?"

"Well, you know my love was always accounting. I went to Washington D.C. to attend university, after that I earned my CPA license and returned to Barbados. The US is not for me; I had to come back home. I'm working in auditing now and it's grueling, but I enjoy it."

"Foot in the door, Pete. Soon from now I'll be hearing that you are the COO of the place. You know you were always a go-getter."

"You know me. I ain't about settling. So what's going on with you these days?"

"What's new with me is that I'm getting married."

"Married? Congratulations, man. When? And who is the lucky woman?"

"Thanks, thanks. Next month is the wedding."

"Good for you. She is Bajan or from one of the other islands?"

"No way. These Bajan and Caribbean women bout here too damn miserable or just want your money."

"Wow, that's a little harsh, Winston. What woman mess you up?"

"Don't pretend like you don't know. All these Caribbean women bout here like to do is nag you, go through your things, and beg for money. I made up my mind five years ago that I done with Bajan and Caribbean women. I met Sasha about a year ago at a party my company had to celebrate a big account we had landed, and we've been talking ever since. It felt right, so I took her out to dinner one night and put an engagement ring on it." Winston pulled up a picture on his cell phone of a smiling milky-skinned, blond-haired woman and proudly thrust it in Peter's face. Peter's eyebrows shot up when he saw the photograph.

"You're surprised that she's white, right?"

"Honestly, I wasn't expecting her to be white."

"That's my girl. White, pretty and drama free."

"So you and Sasha don't have any issues?"

"Not one. In the year that we've been together, we've never fought. White women don't behave like these Bajan women."

"What?" Peter sat forward in his seat and placed his elbows on the table eyeing Winston closely. "Wait a minute. Let me school you on something, Winston. *All* women get miserable at some time, no matter what their color or nationality. Also, the way you treat them could determine the way they behave. You ever thought about that?"

"No matter how good you treat a Bajan woman, she will find something to be miserable about."

"You sound like you had a real bad experience…"

Winston interrupted him. "I'm not basing my knowledge on just one incident. I've had several. All the men I have spoken to who had white and even Asian women said how peaceful and sweet they are compared to Bajan and Caribbean women. Even compared to African American women."

"Boy, you sounding racist. As soon as you bad-talking black women, that is racism on your own kind. You better don't let any black person in New York or in any part of the US hear you."

"It's not about color. This is about women. Women of darker complexions, meaning Caribbean women, are too damn miserable and money hungry. That's my experience."

"Remember what you just said – from *your* experience. I have a beautiful, black, Bajan wife at home and she takes excellent care of me, and I do the same for her. We have a lovely relationship. Now don't get me wrong, we get into some serious arguments sometimes, but that is my wife, and I wouldn't trade her for the world."

"You're a lucky man, and I know I am too, being with a woman who isn't going to give me the kind of trouble the typical Bajan woman will."

"You approaching this thing wrong, hear. And this thing about you never getting into an argument with your fiancée...what if you find yourself in an argument with her *after* you're married? What you going do then?"

"White and Asian women don't like conflict."

"Where you living? They are women. They will always find *something* to fuss about. And if they are unhappy with you, they will fuss even more. You never heard the expression 'Happy wife, happy life?' That saying applies to all women regardless of color or creed."

"I hear you, Peter," Winston said, checking his watch. "Anyway, I gotta run."

"Yeah, man. Good luck. I think you going need it."

"Think what you like. Thanks though," Winston said and tossed back the last of his beer. He and Peter shook hands, and he left the bar. Peter watched him leave and shook his head.

Peter was at Culpepper Bar having a spirited conversation with Nick and a male customer about politics when he saw Winston walk through the door. Winston spotted him right away, and a big smile broke out on his face. Peter didn't return the smile because the last time they had seen each other Winston had pissed him off. He hadn't liked his attitude towards Bajan women at all.

"Hey B. What's happening, man?" Winston shook Peter's hand firmly and they knocked shoulders.

"Could I get a beer?" Winston asked Nick, still smiling broadly.

Nick nodded and turned away to get the drink. The man Peter had been speaking to also retreated.

"How you doing?" Winston asked Peter enthusiastically.

"I'm good. You seem real happy. How has life been?"

"Real good. I can't complain at all. I landed a great job at a communications firm, and I do the marketing and sales for them."

"Good for you. How's married life?"

"Fantastic!"

"How long has it been now?"

"Actually, it was two years ago that you and I saw each other in this bar."

"Yes it was. So the marriage is going fantastic you say? Still no quarrels or issues?"

"Oh, we fuss at each other every now and again, but things are great. She's great."

Peter nodded, impressed that his friend had actually been able to make it work out so well with Sasha. He was waiting for Winston to rub it in his face when Winston rose from his seat and waved to someone. Peter turned his head to see a brown-skinned, chubby-faced woman with a dazzling smile enter the bar.

"Your sister?" Peter casually asked, raising his glass to take a sip of his drink.

"My wife," Winston beamed. "I never did marry Sasha. She was too damn miserable, so I called off the wedding. Then I met Keiron here five months later. Sweetest, coolest woman I have ever met. She lives in New York too. She migrated from Barbados three years ago."

One Cooked Goose

Dianne Weatherhead

Shirleen was on the hunt. She was looking for a rich American man. Based on the five-year plan she had concocted when she left Barbados at age twenty, time was running out. She had one year left to get her trophy husband. That's why she decided to move from Miami, Florida where she had lived with her brother, to Atlanta, Georgia, the epicenter of rap and R&B music in the United States. Soon she would be rubbing shoulders with high-powered music producers and performing artists.

Until then, she had taken a temporary job as a receptionist for a renowned architecture and design firm in the downtown area. Every morning she sashayed across the lobby, the heels of her designer stilettos clicking on the granite floor, her long ponytail weave swinging from side to side like a horse's tail shooing flies, her makeup impeccably applied, and a Coach handbag clasped in her well-manicured hand. Shirleen knew how to draw attention to herself.

"Shirleen, you know you can't afford these expensive things," her brother, Nigel, cautioned whenever she returned from her shopping sprees and hair appointments.

"Listen, that's what credit cards are for," she scoffed. "Soon enough my rich boyfriend will be paying for all these things." Shirleen dismissed her brother's concerns. "You can't get the part if you don't look the part" was her mantra.

One Monday morning, she entered the elevator and pressed the button for the tenth floor.

"Hold the elevator, please." It was Kyle Harrington, the vice president of sales.

"Good morning, Mr. Harrington," she greeted, smoothing an imaginary strand of loose hair behind her ear and unnecessarily adjusting the tight dress that hugged her curvy figure.

"Good morning, Shirleen. I hope you had a good weekend."

"Yes. I hope you did as well," she answered.

"Yes, thank you. A working weekend, but I landed a new client with a half million-dollar budget," he announced, pumping his fist in the air.

"That's great. Congratulations."

When she had first met Kyle, she immediately inquired about his marital status, although he was clearly at least twenty years her senior. "Married with two kids," a co-worker informed her.

The elevator doors slid open to an ultra-modern suite. Kyle swiped his access card to release the locked outer doors which led to a contemporary, high-end designed reception area. Shirleen wished Kyle a good day and prepared herself for the day.

Later in the afternoon, the door buzzer alerted Shirleen to a visitor. Glancing up, she pressed the button at her desk allowing access to a man carrying a large manila envelope.

"Good afternoon, can I help you?" she politely greeted the man she assumed was a courier.

"Good afternoon. I have an appoint..." The man halted mid-sentence. "Shirleen? Shirleen Gaskin? Oh my goodness, you are the last person I expected to see." An unrestrained, dimpled smile transformed his staid demeanor.

Shirleen was as shocked to see Trevor as he was to see her. They had both worked at the Pelican Palms Restaurant in Barbados where she was a sixteen-year-old part-time waitress, and he was a nineteen-year-old cook. Every chance he got, he asked her out on a date, but Shirleen wasn't checking for a cook even though he was a very handsome young man. She had her sights set higher from back then and never gave him the time of day.

"Trevor? Shireen blinked rapidly as if trying to moisten dry contact lenses. "What are you doing in Atlanta? You live here now?"

"Yes, I moved here almost seven years ago," he replied. "You still look as good as you did back in the day, even better actually." Trevor beamed, appreciating what he could see of her behind the desk.

Shirleen quickly appraised him. He too, was still attractive, but instead of the short unkempt afro he wore as a teenager, usually covered by a hairnet, he now sported a sleek, tapered fade haircut and a neatly groomed short beard. She remembered he had dreams of owning his own restaurant on the island's affluent west coast.

"So you have been up here for seven years? Working as a messenger?" Shirleen asked.

"No, I'm not a messenger. I'm still in the restaurant business." He placed the envelope on the sleek, frosted glass countertop.

Her Bajan accent surfaced. "Oh, you still a cook?" she asked, scrunching her nose.

Trevor paused before saying with a twinkle in his eye, "Yes, you could say that. So what about you? I don't see a ring on your finger, so I take it you're not married."

"No I'm not married...yet, but soon enough."

"Maybe we can catch up over lunch or dinner some time."

"Listen Trevor, I'm glad to see you, but if after seven years you is still a cook, you can't do nothing for me now, same as when you couldn't do nothing for me back in Barbados. So let me sign for this package and you can go about your business." Shirleen saw no point in wasting his time or her own.

Trevor's head snapped back at Shirleen's rudeness. He started to respond but was interrupted as she answered an incoming call.

"Good afternoon and thank you for calling Phoenix Architect and Design. How may I direct your call?" she asked, returning to a professional demeanor.

She waved Trevor away expecting him to leave. Instead, he pulled his cell phone from his back pocket and quickly typed a text.

"Why you still here?" she snapped when she hung up from the call.

"Because I have an appointment to see Kyle Harrington," Trevor responded with a cool smile.

Shirleen's eyes almost popped out of their sockets as Kyle entered the reception area.

"Trevor," he said pleasantly, extending his hand. "Thanks for stopping by. Did you bring the information we discussed over the weekend?"

Trevor firmly shook Kyle's hand. Shirleen didn't know what to make of what was unfolding before her.

"Mr. Harrington, you know Trevor?"

"Yes, this is our new client that I mentioned on the elevator. We'll be designing a new restaurant for him. You probably know the one he already owns, White Hibiscus."

Of course she knew White Hibiscus. It was one of the most expensive restaurants in Atlanta, frequented by business executives and entertainers, and known for its masterful fusion of tropical island and Iberian flavors.

"You *own* White Hibiscus?" Shirleen's eye opened wide like saucers. Under her warm-bronze Fenty foundation, her face blanched.

"Yes Shirleen, I do." Trevor smirked, folding his arms across his broad chest.

"But...but...you said you were still a cook."

"Well technically, I'm a chef and I do run my kitchen."

"This young man has an amazing story," Kyle said. "He was discovered by an internationally renowned restaurateur who was visiting Barbados and was so impressed with his style of cooking he hired him on the spot. Then he sent him to culinary schools in New York and Spain."

"Culinary school in Spain?" Shirleen parroted.

"By age twenty-four he had opened his restaurant and the rest, as they say, is history."

"Kyle, let's not bore Shirleen. Why don't we head to your office and get down to some business?"

Shirleen propped her elbows on her desk and rubbed her throbbing temples with her thumbs.

"Shirleen, are you okay?" Kyle asked, concerned. "You look as if you're about to pass out."

"I'm... I'm fine." She managed a forced smile.

Thirty minutes later, Kyle escorted Trevor back to the reception area then returned to his office. Wordlessly, Trevor turned to leave. Before he could open the door, Shirleen slithered sensuously from behind her desk.

"Trevor, if you're still interested in having dinner, I could meet you at your restaurant later this evening," she suggested with aplomb, batting her thick eyelash extensions.

Trevor halted, slowly faced Shirleen and rested his chin on a closed fist in fake contemplation, before flashing his dimpled smile. "You know what Shirleen, you cooked your own goose so good, I could never cook you anything better. So that's a hard pass."

Our Little Secret

Dianne Weatherhead

An errant bedspring jabbed Joselyn in her back as she lay on the thin mattress of the pullout sofa bed in her apartment's living room. "Lord, help me survive these next two weeks," she silently prayed. She couldn't wait to get back to sleeping in her queen-sized bed with its plush memory foam mattress now occupied by her great aunt. It wasn't the uncomfortable sofa bed she needed to survive; it was her Auntie Mavis, who had arrived in New York City a day earlier from Barbados, and already it was one day too many.

From the moment Joselyn picked her up from the airport, a litany of complaints rolled out of the elderly woman's mouth before they even exited the terminal. "The man sitting next to me smell like he allergic to soap, and the pilot land the plane like he just get he license, and why dey ain't got no redcaps to help wid yuh luggage in a big-able American airport?" The fifteen-minute drive from Queens to Brooklyn seemed like an eternity.

Joselyn swung her legs off the bed and stretched to get the kinks out of her aching back. Just as she removed the satin bonnet she wore at night, releasing a mass of shoulder length box braids, Aunt Mavis emerged from the bedroom. Four gray plaits, usually hidden under one of her short, conservatively styled, jet black wigs, pointed in different directions. At age seventy-two, though heavyset, she still carried her frame erect.

"Joselyn? You wake up yet?" As usual Mavis looked like she had just bitten a lime.

"Good morning Auntie Mavis. Yes, I'm up," Joselyn replied, yawning. Trying to maintain a pleasant tone, she asked, "You got a good night's rest?"

"Rest?" Mavis released a long stupse. "All night all I could hear is Parmp! Parmp! Parmp!" she ranted, imitating the blare of car horns. "I barely sleep a wink. People bout here don't sleep?" she grumbled.

That is why they call New York "The City That Never Sleeps" Joselyn thought, but knew better than to verbalize such a response. Instead, she ignored the complaint and headed to the bathroom before making her way to the kitchen to prepare breakfast.

"The French toast will be finished soon," she called out to her aunt who was looking out the front window of the apartment.

"French toast? I don't eat French toast," Mavis informed her niece, wrinkling her nose. "You don't have any cornmeal to make some porridge. If not, you can fry some bakes."

Taking a deep breath, Joselyn removed the heated skillet from the stove and retrieved a package of cornmeal from her pantry.

"So this is the Brooklyn that everybody trying so hard to get to? It look so dingy, like it could use a good scrubbing. And why all the houses the same ugly brown bricks? They don't sell paint up here?"

Joselyn rolled her eyes, sighed, and kept stirring the pot of porridge.

Later that morning, Joselyn showed her aunt around the neighborhood; an enclave of Caribbean immigrants. Within a three-block radius of her apartment, several West Indian eateries, beauty supply shops, hair salons, discount stores, and other small businesses lined the sidewalks. A variety of lilting accents floated in the humid, summer breeze, and island-nation flags proudly fluttered above store awnings. Calypso, zouk and reggae rhythms escaped from the open windows of passing vehicles.

The following day, they took a bus to the train station. Mavis halted at the top of the stairs leading into the subway.

"We have to go down there?" she asked, looking dubiously into the dismal underground entrance.

"It's fine, Auntie Mave," Joselyn patiently assured her.

"Down here look like the bowels of hell to me," Mavis announced as they reached the station platform, "And don't smell much better," she uttered, pinching her nostrils closed.

Joselyn hoped that if she ignored her aunt, she would keep her comments to herself. Fortunately, it wasn't long before the silvery metal train clattered into the dimly lit station.

Joselyn led Mavis to a half empty train car. As they settled onto the dull gray seats, Mavis spotted a squatty woman who had also boarded.

"Have mercy!" Mavis exclaimed. "She musee ain't got no mirrors home, cause I can't believe she left de house looking so on purpose. She mobbaton of pooch like it hollering for murder to get out of dat skirt."

Joselyn's face flushed with embarrassment.

"Auntie Mavis, nobody here cares how anybody looks, and you don't have to comment on everything you see," Joselyn admonished her aunt between clenched teeth.

At the next stop, a pale, blond man with ghoulish facial tattoos and wearing black lipstick and thick dark eyeliner stepped onboard.

"Dracula like he resurrect," Mavis dryly commented.

Joselyn quickly jabbed her aunt in the arm with an elbow. "Shush nuh!"

To her relief, they soon reached their stop in Manhattan. Emerging from the gloomy subway into the bright sunlight, they walked a few blocks to the building where Joselyn had to drop off a package for a friend. A heavy, revolving glass door led them into a cavernous lobby, and then they made their way down a long corridor. Locating the office suite, Joselyn entered a quiet waiting room. Mavis loudly announced, "Good morning" to which none of the seated customers responded.

"People up here don't have no home training? I say 'good morning' and nuhbody ent even unpick dem teeth to answer," she griped.

"Listen, Auntie Mavis. This. Isn't. Barbados," Joselyn hissed, roughly pulling her aunt by the arm back into the hallway. "Everybody just minding their own business and not interested in the next person. A man could walk down the street right now in a diaper and with a monkey on his head and not a soul would bat an eyelash. People are just anonymous and disconnected. That is just the way it is in a big city."

After the unexpected chastisement, Mavis glared at her niece but bit her tongue. For the next few days tension floated between the two women, but it soon dissipated.

Late one evening, Joselyn returned home from work and noticed several shopping bags on an armchair.

"Hi Auntie Mave, you went out on your own today?"

"Yes. I manage to find one of the beauty supply shops and buy a couple new wigs and got some new outfits from a boutique."

"Nice. I'm off from work tomorrow, so we can go to Canal Street. You can get some good deals on handbags."

The next morning, Mavis strutted out of the bedroom sporting a shoulder length honey-brown wig, pink lipstick, and a colorful floral jumpsuit with an off-the-shoulder neckline. Joselyn's eyes opened wide, and her mouth fell open like a broken trapdoor.

"Auntie Mave! You...I...Wow!" she stuttered.

"You like muh new look?" asked Mavis, spinning around. "I always wanted to get a makeover, but you know how people back home always ready to wash their mouth on yuh. So since you tell me that nobody up here care how yuh look, I decide to spruce up muhself for once in muh life. It will be our little secret," she chuckled.

Joselyn nearly fell over. She couldn't remember seeing anything resembling a smile on her aunt's face, much less hearing laughter escape from her lips.

"Okay, it's our little secret," Joselyn agreed, amused by this almost unrecognizable woman as they left the apartment.

As they waited at the bus stop, Mavis and Joselyn were so deep in conversation they didn't notice two women across the street gawking at them.

"Wait, Vernita!" the lanky woman gripped her friend's arm and pointed. "That look like Mavis McCallister."

"Noooo Fayth, that can't be Mavis," said Vernita, peering over her sunglasses as she stared. "Not the Mavis I know."

"Yes girl, it is Mavis! You check the hair and outfit? She come up to America and tink she is a young yam. Where your phone? Take a picture quick. I can't wait to get back to Barbados and show it to the usher board at church."

Her Perfect American Guy

Suzanne Durant

Five feet six inches. Creamy brown skin. Slim and curvy with a nice butt and perky breasts. Naturally curly hair falling just below the shoulders. Big brown eyes and long eyelashes. Tianna twisted and twirled herself in front of the mirror, loving everything she was seeing. Changing more than twenty times, she struck different poses trying to figure out which outfit she was going to wear to the mall. She had to look just right for the admiring stares she knew she would receive from men, but more importantly, she had to look perfect for all the selfies she planned to take and send to her boyfriend, JC, who lived in the United States.

She returned to her large closet that housed several trendy outfits purchased during her annual visits to New York, growing increasingly impatient with her failed efforts to locate the perfect outfit for her outing. Just then, she heard three loud honks from a car pulling into the parking lot of her apartment complex. Grabbing a robe, she walked into the living room and peeped through her window. It was her good friend Tracia. She ran down the hall and opened the door just as Tracia was alighting from her car.

"Wait," Tracia said, seeing Tianna in the robe when she made it to the door. "Why you can't be ready whenever I come to pick you up?"

"You say that all the time," Tianna said and stupsed, then turned around and headed back to her bedroom. "You don't get tired saying it?"

"Look, just put on something and let's go. You act as if we going to a fashion show. We just going to the mall."

"It's not my fault that I have more style than merely jeans and tee-shirts."

"I'll have you know that these jeans are Spragee and this top is not a tee-shirt," Tracia said, popping her shirt at the shoulders as she followed Tianna into the bedroom.

"Just help me find something to wear. I have to send pictures to JC."

"Seriously Tee, you still talking to him?'

"He's perfect like me, so why wouldn't I talk to him?"

"You have never even met the man or heard his voice. And this is going on what? Two years now?"

"Just a year and a half. But JC gets me, and I get him."

"What is there to get about someone you've never met? And how do you even know he is who he says he is and lives in the US? He might be some scam artist in Thailand or Timbuktu trying to get money off you."

"I'll have you know that he lives in Washington, D.C. and he's never asked for money."

"Not yet."

"Well, after six months and he has not asked, chances are he won't ask."

"So you say. We got plenty of good Bajan men around though. Why you need someone from outside?"

"How many times do I have to tell you that I don't want a Bajan man. They have no class, and they don't know how to treat women, especially a good one like me. Plus, things in America are better. The men are better looking, the clothes are better and cheaper. America has all I need."

Tracia rolled her eyes. "I love you like a sister right, but you need to stop this foolishness about Bajan men and America. America is not all that; they got bare issues over there. And just because this JC is from America does not mean that he is classy, better, or even real. There are a lot of crazy men out there, and these dating sites are like fodder for them."

"Oh brother, you are sssooo dramatic," Tianna sighed and rolled her eyes while pulling on a low-cut blouse and a short, white denim skirt and then donning a pair of strappy sandals. She carefully examined herself in the mirror.

After a couple of twirls in the four-inch heels, she smiled and picked up her handbag. "Let's go."

Tracia followed, shaking her head.

That night, Tianna stayed up messaging back and forth on her phone with JC. He was expressing an interest in seeing her and lamenting that his camera was not working. Then, he made a suggestion.

> JC: You know what? Why don't I come and see you?

> Tianna: Will you really be able to make it this time?

> JC: I promise. Last time I had some challenges with my work schedule, but this time I should be able to make it so I can see your beautiful face.

> Tianna: That would be great. How soon can you get here?

> JC: I would love to come as soon as possible, but there's one small obstacle I'm sure we can fix.

> Tianna: What's that?

> JC: I don't have the money for the trip. I've been saving from the modeling jobs I've been doing but it hasn't been enough to get me a plane ticket to Barbados. Do you think you could send some and I'll put it with what I have to get the ticket?

"He might be some scam artist in Thailand or Timbuktu trying to get money off you or something," Tracia's words echoed in Tianna's head. She had confidently told Tracia he hadn't ever asked her for money, yet here he was now asking. Could her sweet American guy be just like the Bajan men she had encountered after all?

> Tianna: How about if I came to see you?

There was a thirty-second pause before JC answered and when he did, he started typing, then stopped, then started again.

> JC: You know what? That sounds like a great idea. Have you ever been to DC?

> Tianna: As you know I'm a New York girl so this will be my first time in DC.

> JC: Well how soon can you get here?

Tracia sat in the airport lounge with Tianna waiting for their first flight to the US to be called. They had to fly to Miami first and then from there take a connecting flight to Ronald Reagan National Airport in Washington D.C. She could not believe she had let Tianna talk her into accompanying her on what she saw as a wild ride to the US to chase behind a man she had never met.

"I mean, we're already at the damn airport, but I have to ask you again – are you crazy?"

"Crazy in love with my perfect American guy."

"Tianna, just because it's made in America doesn't mean it's great. They even get most of their stuff from China anyway."

"Stop being silly, Tracia. We're on our way to meet my man. We'll have a great time. Who knows? A year from now I might be moving to America once this meeting goes well."

Tracia's jaw dropped to the floor as she looked at her friend's beaming face. All she could do was shake her head and prepare herself for whatever awaited them in D.C.

When they arrived at the Airbnb Tianna had booked, Tianna messaged JC to make arrangements to meet. Right after sending the message, her phone rang highlighting the same number she had just sent a message to. Tianna was surprised and suddenly felt nervous about taking the call.

"Hello?" she answered tentatively.

"Hi Tianna. It's JC." A deep smooth voice floated through the phone.

"H-Hi," Tianna found herself responding shyly. She never expected JC to call her since all their communication had been by messaging, so hearing his voice was a complete surprise. He sounded so damn sexy too.

"Hey baby," the voice rumbled. "It is so good to hear your voice."

"Oh wow, it's so good to hear yours too."

"I see you made it. I would have met you at the airport, but I don't have a car."

"That's ok." Tianna found herself so enthralled with the voice over the phone, she could barely speak.

The voice suggested they meet that night at a restaurant that he said was just ten minutes walking distance from where Tianna was staying.

"I can't wait until tomorrow to see you, baby," the voice said.

"Me either. I'll be there."

Just as Tiana hung up from the call and fell backwards on the bed with a huge smile on her face, Tracia came out of the bathroom breathing heavily.

"Damn, I don't know what I ate today but it definitely was in a hurry to get out."

"Please, spare me the details, woman," Tianna said, holding her nose even though Tracia had closed the door.

"Did you hear from your perfect guy?"

"Actually, I did. I just hung up from a call with him."

"Really? What did he sound like? What did he have to say?"

"Ooohhh Tracia, he sounds so good. He has this sexy, deep voice, and it sent chills right through me," Tianna gushed, clutching the phone to her chest as she laid on her back. "He wants us to meet tonight at a restaurant not too far from here."

"Well, well, well," Tracia said, grinning and rubbing her hands together. "So we are about to meet the elusive JC. It's about time."

Tianna had agreed to meet JC at 7:00 p.m. and by 6:30 she and Tracia were out the door, making it to the restaurant ten minutes before the agreed-on time.

"*This* is what you call a restaurant?" Tracia snorted. "It's a damn diner. You mean he found the cheapest place to take you for a first date?"

"Shut up and leave my man alone," Tianna said dismissively. She chose a table where she could sit and see every person who entered the diner.

"Well, if you like it, I love it," Tracia rolled her eyes and turned her attention to the menu.

By 7:30, eight couples, three groups of people, a few unaccompanied women, two youngsters Tianna guessed to be about thirteen or fourteen, and several lone men had entered the diner, but no one approached their table. By this time,

Tracia was not only getting impatient, but also ravenously hungry.

"Just as I suspected," she snarled, gesturing to the waitress so she could order. She was not planning to waste any more time waiting for JC.

"He'll be here," Tianna calmly said.

Just then, a tall, dark-skinned, athletically built man entered the diner. Tianna gasped and when he looked at her and broke into a smile, she smiled back, hardly able to sit still in her seat.

"He's here," she said eagerly. Tracia looked around to see Tianna's mystery man.

The man strode purposefully in Tianna's direction, showing beautiful white teeth, and walked right past them to join a man seated behind them. Tracia saw the hurt and crestfallen look on her friend's face and felt bad for her. Just as she was about to try comforting her, Tianna's phone buzzed. A message from JC appeared.

> JC: My sweet Tianna, I am so sorry but I cannot make it. My mother is ill and I have to take her to the hospital.

> Tianna: OMG I'm so sorry to hear that. I hope it's not too serious.

> JC: I hope not too but we'll see what the doctor says. Again I am so sorry. I was dressed and ready to come meet you

> when this happened. Can we meet tomorrow instead?

> Tianna: Of course.

They agreed to meet the following day at the Lincoln Memorial at 1:00 p.m. and then find somewhere to have lunch.

> Tianna: I have my friend with me. Is it ok if she comes with us?

> JC: She can have lunch with us but will she be spending the entire day with us? I want to spend the day with just you.

> Tianna: Ok. No problem. After lunch she can return to the house. We can be together. Just the two of us.

> JC: Great. I love you, my love. Can't wait to see you. Sleep well.

> Tianna: I love you too. Can't wait to see you either. I hope all is well with your mother.

"Of course he's not coming," Tracia said when Tianna looked up at her.

After Tianna told Tracia that JC's mother was ill and they had agreed to meet at the Lincoln Memorial Center, Tracia released a stupse.

"What is your problem now?" Tianna snapped.

"You honestly believe whoever that was that messaged you?"

"You need to stop being so skeptical. Didn't you just hear that his mother is sick? How can I expect the man to come meet me when his mother is sick?"

Tracia was about to repeat her disbelief in JC's existence and reprimand Tianna for her gullibility but held her tongue and simply said, "Ok."

"After the Lincoln Memorial we're going to lunch, but after lunch you have to make yourself scarce so JC and I can spend some quality time together."

Tracia snorted and shook her head. "You really expect me to disappear and leave you with someone we don't know anything about?"

"I know JC. We've been talking for over a year."

"Sending messages back and forth to an invisible man is not talking, and it sure as hell isn't a relationship. And just because you've heard his voice doesn't make him real."

"Look, you have been giving me a hard time about all this since you agreed to come with me. Why the hell did you come?"

"I'm still asking myself that question," Tracia sighed. "Look, let's order some food, eat, and head back to the house. It's been a long day and I just want to get some sleep."

Tracia looked at her watch and sighed loudly. It was five minutes before two, and she and Tianna were still sitting on the steps of the Lincoln Memorial waiting for JC to show up. To fill the time, Tianna had been searching on her phone for all the malls and shops they could visit as she had a laundry list of clothes she wanted to buy.

"This is a complete waste of time," Tracia lamented, and not for the first time. "We need to leave."

"He's running a little late. Where's your patience?" Tianna said cheerfully.

"OMG Tianna. He promised to visit you in Barbados and had a convenient excuse for not being able to make it. Then, after flying our asses all the way here, he made plans to meet us last night and didn't show up. Can't you see you're being catfished?" Tracia had felt sorry for Tianna last night, but not today sitting around in the heat waiting for a no-show.

Tianna frowned at her friend. "No way would JC catfish me. *Have you seen me?* Plus, this is America. The men here are not like the men at home."

All the *Catfish* television shows Tracia had watched flooded her mind, and she glared at her friend, trying to resist the urge to slap her.

"There are good things about America, but Ms. Lady, in case you are too naïve to be aware, one of the many negative things about America is the scams, and relationship scams are one of the most common."

"Look," Tianna said, losing patience with Tracia, "you don't have to stick around here with me, you know. If you are going to be like this, you can leave."

"Oh, I'm leaving all right. Leaving and heading straight to the airport. I done with you and this foolishness."

"We going shopping later, right?" Tianna quipped.

Tracia shook her head and walked off in a huff, heading for the train station. Less than five minutes later she heard someone behind her.

"Tracia, wait!"

Turning around, she saw Tianna sprinting toward her and waving her arms in the air. Tracia's first instinct was to take off running too since it looked like Tianna was being chased, but she stood her ground and braced herself to fight just in case Tianna really was trying to get away from some kind of danger, like this JC person, if he were indeed real.

"Someone chasing you?" she asked when Tianna was just a few feet away.

"No, no, no! I coming with you."

"So why were you running like the police chasing you? Where's your do-no-wrong American man?"

"Seconds after you left, a youngster approached me telling me he is JC's little brother. I am looking at this little boy and thinking how familiar he looks, but I can't place him. Then he tells me that JC is at the hospital with their mother, and they need some help paying her medical bill and if I could please come and help them out."

"Wha?" Tracia gasped.

"And then it hit me. Two young boys walked into the diner last night. He was one of them. Trace, I hate to admit it, but you were right about it being a scam. Them two young boys was messing with me. Leh we get the hell out of here."

"I with you," Tracia smiled, quickening her pace. "Straight to the airport and back home."

Tianna raised her eyebrow at Tracia. "Straight to what airport? We got some shopping to do first. The only JC I looking to spend my money on is J.C. Penney. Leh we go girl."

Lost in Translation

Dianne Weatherhead

Waveney flipped the wall calendar page to July and tacked it back onto the fabric-covered partition of her cubicle. The picture of a vibrant tropical sunset over Brandon's Beach brought back childhood memories of Saturdays spent splashing in the crystal-clear waters and hours playing on the fine, white sand.

"Waveney." Her thoughts were interrupted by Jerry McDuffy, the data center manager, who had a petite, young woman in tow. "I want to introduce you to Pamela. Today is her first day with the company."

"Nice to meet you, and welcome," Waveney said politely in her refined, but distinctively Barbadian accent.

"Thank you," Pamela replied brusquely. She appeared to be in her late twenties, her straightened hair stylishly cut in an asymmetrical bob.

You betta check that attitude at the door, Waveney thought.

"If you can show her around the office and get her settled in, I would really appreciate it," said Jerry. "I just got called into a meeting with the I.T. department."

"No problem," Waveney agreed.

"Okay Pamela, you're in good hands. You ladies have a great day," Jerry said, as he left the area.

Waveney supervised the data entry operators, a job she had held for the past seven years and the reason she had relocated from New York City to Connecticut. She was well-liked by her co-workers who knew of her strong connection to her island home. Some even called her the unofficial Barbados ambassador and joked that if Waveney were cut, she would bleed mauby, a traditional beverage no respectable Bajan home would be found without.

As she stepped towards Pamela, Waveney noticed the employee ID badge clipped onto the waistband of the young woman's trendy skirt.

"Your surname is Roachford?" Waveney asked. "You're from Barbados by any chance?" It was a common surname on the island.

Pamela curtly corrected Waveney's Bajan pronunciation in a heavily intonated American accent. "It is Roch-ford, not Roach-furd. And yes, I am from Barbados."

Waveney's jaw tightened. *Seriously? Since when R...o...a...c ...h is Roch. The 'A' must be get arrested and have the right to remain silent or something.* She mused. "Oh, okay. I'm from there, too." She was usually excited to meet a fellow Bajan and exchange information to find out if they had any mutual acquaintances. This time was very different.

"Yes, I can tell." Pamela gave a side-eye glance at Waveney's desk noting a mug emblazoned with "Bajan Fuh Life," a mouse pad customized with the blue and yellow national flag of Barbados and a screensaver on the computer monitor displaying costumed revelers during the island's annual Kadooment parade.

Waveney noticed Pamela's aloof attitude, but nonetheless tried to engage her in conversation. "So how long have you lived here? It's almost twenty-three years for me."

And you still sound like you just stepped out of a canefield. I don't understand you people that don't try to better yourselves, Pamela thought before she blandly blurted, "Two years."

Waveney's eyebrow arched. *Two years? You now land and have more American twang than the Yankees who were born and bred here.* "Have you been back since you left? I've only missed returning two years since I've been living here; in 2001 after the World Trade Center attack, and 2020 when Covid hit and shut down everything."

Well good for you. Pamela's upper lip tightened. *Why would I want to go back there every year? As if I'm missing something.* "No, I haven't been back since I left. I prefer to explore other parts of the world and see more exciting places," she replied, checking her watch.

Awrighty then. Waveney was now convinced that Pamela was a real poppit. She knew not everyone felt the need to display their cultural identity as ardently as she did, but this woman made it sound as if Barbados were a leper colony that needed to be avoided at all cost.

"Let me show you around the office," *and then get you out of my eyesight.*

At home later that evening, Waveney's husband asked about her day as they prepared dinner. Waveney entertained him with the tale of meeting the new hire. "It's Roch...ford," she perfectly mimicked Pamela's nasal, pseudo-American accent, followed by a cough-inducing laugh. Regaining her composure, Waveney said, "The girl acts like she went to the best surgeon and had every iota of Bajan liposuctioned out of her body. Cuh-dear. Poor soul."

As the weeks rolled by, Waveney maintained cordial interactions with Pamela and resisted mentioning anything Bajan-related to her.

During lunch one afternoon, Waveney's Jamaican co-worker, Junella joined her at a table in the breakroom.

"Are you going to the Caribbean Music Festival next week? Beres Hammond is performing." Junella closed her eyes and started swaying, as if hearing the Jamaican reggae artist singing one of his lovers-rock ballads.

"You know that isn't going to miss me. I can't wait to see Krosfyah," Waveney answered, referring to the popular Bajan soca band.

"I have an extra ticket." Junella shifted towards the adjacent table where Pamela sat. "Pamela, are you interested in going to the Caribbean Music Festival?"

Pamela didn't look up from the magazine she was flipping through. "No, thank you. I don't go to *those* types of events," she replied haughtily.

"Eh eh!" Junella turned back to face Waveney, mouth agape. "Wha she mean by that?" Her rhythmic accent more evident than before.

Pamela exhaled deeply. "I'm more into events like Coachella."

Cow-chella indeed. Coach-cella with the silent 'A'. Waveney barely held back a chuckle at the feign inflection. "Don't even bother your head with her. We'll have a good time as usual." She checked the wall clock. "Anyway, I have to get back to work."

Waveney was intently preparing a report when she heard a loud thud emanate from the direction of the lunchroom and saw Jerry dash from his nearby office. Several minutes later he reappeared looking frazzled and flummoxed.

Waveney motioned him over to her cubicle. "Jerry, what happened?"

Jerry smoothed back the few strands of red hair from his flushed forehead. "Oh my goodness. Pamela slipped and fell in the lunchroom," he gushed. "She says she's okay, but I think we should call 911."

"Why? Is she bleeding? Something broken?"

"No, but I think she may have hit her head and possibly has a concussion."

"Why would you think that?"

"She started babbling strange things about her pets."

"Her pets?"

"Yes, she said something about her cat Spraddle, and that she broke her pooch. But who breaks a dog? Then, when she saw her skirt was torn, she kept asking for a sandwich."

"A sandwich?"

"Yes, cheese on bread to be exact. Sounds like a concussion to me."

A cackle erupted from Waveney before she clamped her hand over her mouth. Jerry looked blankly at Waveney, scratching his head.

"It's okay Jerry, nothing is wrong with Pamela. She'll be fine. She just remembered where she came from and took a quick 'trip' back there." Another belly laugh escaped as Waveney dabbed the tears streaming down her cheeks. She wasn't sure which was more amusing: Pamela's sudden unearthing of her Bajan roots or poor Jerry lost in translation.

Tech Me Home

Suzanne Durant

"A supermarket or mall within walking distance?" Eleanor asked as she reached for the milk to pour into her tea.

She had arrived in Washington, D.C. two days earlier from Barbados for a two-week visit with her only son, Ronnie and daughter-in-law, Vanelle. The last time she had been in the US was ten years ago to visit a friend in Brooklyn and then, she had only stayed for one week. Ronnie and Vanelle on the other hand, had traveled back and forth almost yearly for over fifteen years since Ronnie left at age nineteen to study in the US. Eleanor, a teacher, had one more year to go before retirement and was seriously considering moving to live with them. She had made this trip to get a feel for life in the US.

Though Ronnie and Vanelle had tried to get vacation for the first week of Eleanor's visit, they had not been successful as Ronnie was leading a special engineering project for which he had to be on-site daily, and Vanelle was very busy with a new and demanding client at the accounting firm where she worked.

Ronnie and Vanelle usually left the house by 8:00 a.m., so to spend some time with them, Eleanor had risen early, something she was accustomed to, and cooked breakfast. She knew she would not see them again until much later that night, which was not a problem for her because she kept herself occupied by sleeping, reading, and watching television, things she hardly got a chance to do when she was home.

"The closest supermarket and mall are a twenty to thirty-minute drive. Walking will take much longer," Vanelle said while munching on a piece of toast.

"Leave a car for me then. I have no problem driving. Just give me directions," Eleanor said, pleased with the enthusiastic way her children were digging into her breakfast. But suddenly, they stopped eating and looked at her as though she had been speaking gibberish.

"You sure you're up for driving, Mum?" Ronnie asked. This is Washington, D.C. not St. Michael. There's a different system here with a bunch of one-way streets and highways that have traffic flow reversal and lots of detours."

"You talking to me as if I am the child and you are the parent. The fact that I drive perfectly well at home should mean that

I can handle myself here. A road is a road. The two of you go along to work and leave a car for me so I can go and do some shopping."

"I can take you when I get back home, Mum," Vanelle offered.

"I don't want you rushing home to take me out. I'll be fine. I just don't want to be sitting around in the house all day. Just tell me how to get there."

"I can tell you how to get there, but it will be so much easier if you use the navigation system in Vanelle's car," Ronnie said before pushing his last forkful of scrambled eggs into his mouth.

Vanelle kicked her husband's leg under the table before turning to Eleanor. "Mum, when you leave this development, make a right onto the main road out front and stay on it. It is one straight road. Take your time. You should see DealMart on the right, a warehouse style store that sells clothes, household items, food, whatever you need. Just look out for the sign. You can't miss it."

"Once it is one straight road, I will find it," Eleanor said. "Now last night I was looking for your phone book. Where do you all keep it?"

Ronnie couldn't help himself; he burst out laughing.

"What is the joke? Vanelle, why he laughing so?"

"Mummy, I don't mean anything by it," Ronnie said after settling down. "We don't use phone books, not when you can access whatever information you want on your phone. Here, let me show you." Ronnie picked up his phone. "What do you need?"

"Look, this is too much technology for me," Eleanor grumbled, not making any effort to look at her son's phone with him.

If there was one thing Eleanor was not, it was a fan of technology. As far as she was concerned there was too much dependence on the internet, and people were relying too much on technology to do things for them. She believed in talking directly to people; that way you could get better assistance and a personal touch.

"Ronnie, just write down the number for Mum. Don't confuse her by showing her anything on your phone."

"I have another question. Where the phone?"

"I'll get one for you this evening Mum, before I come home," Ronnie said.

"I don't mean a cell phone. I mean a house phone. Where do you all keep it? I checked the kitchen and the front house and didn't see it."

"I'm afraid we don't have one," Vanelle jumped in before Ronnie could respond.

"Wait, no phone book and no house phone? How the hell wunna does operate in here?" Eleanor exclaimed.

"Lots of people in the US don't bother with landlines anymore because they have cell phones. Why have a landline that we will never use?" Ronnie reasoned.

"When we get back home, you can use mine or Ronnie's to make the call, Mum. Who do you want to call?" Vanelle asked.

"I just want to see about staying an extra week, if it's okay with you two."

"Of course. You don't even have to ask," Ronnie said, rising from his seat and kissing his mother on the cheek before grabbing his work bag. Vanelle took one last sip of her coffee and also grabbed her laptop bag after pecking Eleanor on the cheek.

"Why you telling your mother about a navigation system in the car? You know she's not interested in no technology. She complains about emails and internet banking," Vanelle whispered as she and Ronnie walked to the front door.

"Yeah. I wasn't thinking. But if she intends to do more driving on her own, she needs to know how to use it. I will teach her."

"I leaving that to you. I doubt she is interested in learning anything so," Vanelle said. "Oh, Mum!" she turned and shouted just before stepping out the door. "The keys to my car are on the side table here by the door. Remember to drive on the right side of the road. Oh, and put gas in the car. I'm leaving $30 under the car keys. There's a gas station just around the corner."

I gotta put gas in it too? Eleanor grumbled to herself but cheerfully responded to Vanelle with, "Ok. Thanks."

It was still early, so Eleanor leisurely finished her breakfast and went back upstairs to shower and dress. After slipping on a pair of jeans, a white blouse, and sneakers, an hour later Eleanor picked up her handbag, along with the car keys and the money, and headed out the door.

"Hm," she murmured, looking at her daughter-in-law's 2021 Ford SUV carefully for the first time. A small dose of intimidation hit Eleanor because she drove an older model, no-frills Toyota sedan at home. Nevertheless, she shook off her fear and got into the vehicle.

"This dashboard look like a damn cockpit," she said as she eyed the various controls, but she took a moment to familiarize herself with the basics. She reversed out of the driveway and carefully made her way onto the main road while repeating in her head, 'Keep to the right, keep to the right.' Just as Vanelle said, the gas station was a few yards outside of the residential area where they lived, so Eleanor pulled into the station and parked next to a pump. Two minutes passed and she noticed that no one was coming to her; in fact, the few drivers who were at the gas station were pumping their own gas. Eleanor got out of the car and approached the man at the pump next to her.

"Uh, hello," she began. "Do you know if there are any gas attendants around?"

"No ma'am. Do you need some help?"

"Actually yes. This is my first time at a gas station here."

"Are you paying by cash, credit card or Apple Pay?"

"Apple Pay? I don't even know what that is. I use cash for everything."

The man asked her to wait a moment while he completed filling up his car, then he took her inside the small convenience store to the clerk so she could pay, and they returned to her car where he offered to pump the gas for her. Eleanor was like a fish out of water trying to find the release clip inside the car to open the gas tank until her guardian angel showed her how to open it from the outside. With a gentle poke, the cover of the gas tank flipped open to reveal the opening where the nozzle was to be inserted. Eleanor was alarmed at the lack of security around the gas tank but held her tongue while making a note to bring it up with Ronnie that night. She thanked the man for all his help and climbed back into the vehicle.

"How they don't have people pumping your gas for you? Bare foolishness," Eleanor grumbled as she pulled out of the station onto the main road, which was not very busy. Following Vanelle's instructions, she drove slowly looking out for the DealMart sign.

Just then, she heard a car horn toot behind her.

I just come bout here the other day and somebody tooting at me? I don't know nobody bout here, she thought as she stuck her hand out the window and waved at the person in the car behind her. Eleanor was accustomed to greeting and being greeted by people she knew in Barbados with a toot of the horn. She was pleasantly surprised that Americans practiced the same courtesy.

The person tooted again, and again Eleanor waved thinking they had not seen her first wave of hello. This time, her gesture was greeted with a more aggressive honk, which Eleanor finally and correctly deciphered as *You are driving too damn slow. Get out of the way.* Eleanor, sufficiently flustered by the intensity of the motorist, pulled onto the shoulder of the road so that impatient driver, and about ten others that she seemed to have been holding up, could pass her. After making sure the road was clear, Eleanor returned onto it with a death grip on the steering wheel. She sighed with relief when she finally saw her destination a short distance ahead of her. She turned into the parking lot saying to herself, *It's a good thing I didn't have far to go.*

She entered the large shopping facility and became excited at all the purchasing possibilities in front of her. Eleanor took her time wandering through the aisles looking at clothes and household items and marveling at the prices before making her way to the grocery section. After completing her shopping, she sought out an available cashier. Eleanor grew alarmed as she walked along the line of cashier stations to find every one of them empty.

"Where the ass are the cashiers?" she muttered.

At the end of the line of eight empty cashier stations was a large area marked "Self-checkout." Eleanor slapped her forehead with the palm of her hand and shook her head. In Barbados, a few of the supermarkets had implemented self-service registers, but the cashier stations were still very much in operation, and she was one of many Barbadians who still preferred human interaction. This was why she still did all of her banking at a teller's window and always made sure she spoke to an operator whenever she made a call to a business. In DealMart, there was no avoiding using a self-checkout station.

Eleanor actually thought about leaving her overflowing cart right there and returning home, but changed her mind and reluctantly entered the scan-and-go arena. She twirled around for a couple seconds before approaching one of the digital registers. She looked around to see how other customers were checking their items, disgusted at the fact that she also had to bag her things herself, and copied their actions. When she had to check out the fruits and vegetables, that was it for Eleanor. Unaware of how to ring them up, she became frustrated. At that point, she really felt like leaving the cart and seeing if Vanelle would bring her back when she came home from work. Looking around, Eleanor saw a young store employee and wasted no time in calling him over.

"Help me here, chile," she said.

"Yes, ma'am." The young man proceeded to tell her what to do. Eleanor looked at him like he had gone mad.

"Is something wrong, ma'am?"

"Chile, just check the rest of stuff for me and tell me how to pay because me and these hi-tech things don't 'gree." The young man smiled and obliged. After he had taken care of her, Eleanor walked towards the exit.

"Ma'am, your groceries," the attendant said, pushing the cart towards her.

"You not bringing them to my car?" Eleanor asked, her hands on her hips.

"That's not my job ma'am...but I'll do it for you."

Eleanor finally made it home, exhausted from her unwelcomed baptism with technology. After putting away the food items, she relaxed with a snack for an hour, prepared dinner, then finally settled down in front of the television for the rest of the day. When Ronnie and Vanelle made it home that night, they all sat at the dinner table to enjoy the meal of stewed chicken, basmati rice and vegetables.

"One thing I really miss about you, Mum, is your cooking," Ronnie said between mouthfuls. "I glad you planning to stay an extra week. I really looking forward to more of these meals."

"Me too," Vanelle chimed in. "Let me know when you ready to call the airline, Mum."

"I going have to teach you how to cook like me, Vanelle, because I plan to leave my departure date right where it is. I getting old; I need somebody to pump my gas and carry out my groceries for me, boh. Seeing you two is nice, but life for me is at home in my sweet, little Barbados. You two can continue visiting me from now on."

Back in Time

Dianne Weatherhead

Can't wait to see you next Sunday! I have everything planned and my guest room is ready for you.

Monday - *Times Square and Madame Tussaud's Museum to check out Ri Ri's wax figure, then a Broadway show.*

> **Tuesday** - we going to shop like shopping going out of style. We heading to Garden State Mall in New Jersey that nearly twice as big as the whole of Bridgetown...300 stores and no sales tax on clothes.

> **Wednesday** - your feet gine feel like they drop off from walking the mall, so we chilling at home.

> **Thursday** - we will play by ear.

> **Friday** - Spa Day - facials, massages, sauna, mud wraps, the works.

> And **Saturday**, your big day, is a surprise. All I will say is dress to impress. Wish you could stay longer than a week though.

Natalie finished reading her best friend, Talia's, text and broke into a spontaneous song. Her narrow shoulders bounced to the syncopated soca rhythm of her rendered version of the birthday song, and her neat locs danced as her head twisted from side to side.

"Happy birthday to me!
I soon turning thirty.
And heading to New York City,
To party and spree."

Her hands shook so much with excitement that her fingers could barely type her response.

> "Wuhloss!! Gonna be the best week EVER! The countdown is on. T minus 7 days!"

Four days later, as she put the small suitcase she had started packing into a larger empty one, (she knew she would need a second bag for all the planned shopping) Natalie's phone pinged.

> "Nat, so sorry to tell you but plans have changed. Hubby and I have contracted COVID and we sick as dogs. See if you can reschedule your vacation. I know you put in for it months ago and your boss isn't the most cooperative person. Sorry sweetheart. I feel so terrible."

Natalie could not contain the tears that streamed down her face as she replied, telling Talia to feel better soon and would call her later. Then she called her mother and explained her predicament.

"Don't make no moves yet," her mother tried to reassure her. "I think you have two cousins on your father's side in Long Island that might be able to help. Let me see if I can get hold of them."

Within two hours, Natalie had a place to stay with cousins she had never met, but according to her mother, they seemed happy to accommodate her and show her around. Hopefully she could salvage her birthday trip.

"Talia, you won't believe where I am and what I'm doing," Natalie whispered into her cell phone while standing in a quiet corner of a large room with people milling around. She was waiting for her cousins to return from the restroom.

"Girl, instead of visiting the wax figure museum with you, I here at a museum looking at old dinosaur bones." Natalie paused as she heard Talia giggling. "I glad you think it funny."

"Sorry Nat, I don't mean to laugh," she said with the titter still in her voice.

"Don't get me wrong, I really appreciate Ruby and Pearl being so hospitable, but if I wanted to look at old bones I coulda stay home and look at the ones my neighbor's pot starver dog always dropping at my back door. I ain't come up here for no educational trip."

"When you said you were staying with cousins, I assumed they were around our age. But retired nurses? I feel for you."

"Girl, I was surprised when these elderly twin sisters meet me at the airport. But my father was the last of twelve children and their mother was the eldest of the siblings, so that explains the age difference. Anyway, they coming. I gone. Talk later." Natalie hurriedly ended the call.

"Phew!" Ruby sighed with relief, patting her stomach. "I needed that pitstop. Nat, you enjoyed the exhibitions?"

"Oh yeah, beyond anything I could have imagined." She faked a broad smile.

"I'm so glad you enjoyed yourself. Let's pick up something to eat and have lunch in the park near the house," Pearl suggested.

Long Island was not a bustling, energetic city like Brooklyn where Talia lived. Pearl and Ruby resided in a quiet suburban town with limited public transportation. Their house was on a wide lot with a grassy backyard. Beautiful flowering shrubs and rose bushes bordered the front and sides of the house. They loved gardening and were excited to take Natalie to a botanical garden and flower show the day after the museum trip.

"Talia, if I hear bout phalaenopsis or dendrobiums, or bout putting an ice cube on your orchid ever again, I gine lose my mind. Thank goodness I finally going to a mall tomorrow to do some shopping. My cousins really wanted to come with me, but I insisted they just drop me off in the morning and pick me up in the evening. No offense to my family, but you could imagine what they would want me to buy?" she said to her friend. "I would look like I went shopping at the Geriatric Fashion House." The girls laughed, then wished each other good night.

The following evening, after a satisfying day of shopping, Natalie stood outside the mall at the agreed pick-up point, ladened with shopping bags, when Pearl and Ruby pulled up.

After putting everything into the trunk, she climbed into the back seat and slipped her shoes off her aching feet.

"How was it?" Pearl asked, looking back at Natalie.

"Fantastic. I found lots of great stuff at prices that suit my pocket perfectly. That mall has some good sales. I must come back again before I leave," Natalie said, all the while smiling proudly. She filled them in on bargains she got from Victoria's Secret, Macy's, and the other stores on the short ride to their house.

"Well, we hope you found something special to wear," Ruby said as she pulled the car into her driveway.

"To wear where?"

The three hopped out of the car, and as they unloaded Natalie's packages, Pearl said, "Natalie, we know your birthday is coming up, so to celebrate we got tickets to a fete one of the Bajan associations is having on Saturday."

"A fete?" Natalie perked up. It looked like things were taking a turn for the better and she would have a birthday to remember after all.

"Thank you!" She hugged Pearl then Ruby. She really thought she was going to spend her birthday watching NCIS and nursing a bottle of wine by herself.

On Saturday evening, Natalie twisted her locs together and secured them atop her head allowing a few to trail down her bare shoulders exposed by the halter top of a sleek, hot pink jumpsuit. She slipped on a pair of stylish iridescent strappy heels, not too high, as she intended to dance the night away, hopefully with a handsome guy...or guys. She planned on turning some heads tonight. Long silver earrings, a silver necklace with a small heart-shaped pendant, and a thick silver bangle completed her outfit. After checking her makeup to make sure it popped just the way she liked it, she took a few selfies and posted them to her Instagram account.

Pearl and Ruby appeared, both dressed in flowy chiffon tops, one in red, the other in blue, black slacks, and low wedge-heeled silver shoes.

A taxi arrived just after 8:00 p.m. to transport them to the venue, an elegant reception hall with hundreds of twinkling fairy lights illuminating the exterior. Double glass doors opened into a wide, marbled foyer where a huge crystal chandelier cast an enchanting golden glow. Natalie was impressed by the grandeur. She was sure the evening would be spectacular and she would definitely have a birthday to remember.

Tall blue and gold balloon towers flanked the entrance to a large, high-ceiling room. Inside, tables festooned in black tablecloths and blue and yellow floral centerpieces edged the perimeter of the polished hardwood floor, where several older ladies and men were paired off dancing to the classic calypso *Hit It* by the Mighty Gabby.

Pearl and Ruby excused themselves to mingle with friends they had spotted. *I guess the younger crowd will be arriving later,* Natalie thought, as she took a seat and surveyed the room.

An hour later, Natalie still sat at the table, her chin propped on her up-turned palm, watching senior couples circling the floor and trying to ignore the elderly gentleman in a vibrant yellow suit and matching fedora at the next table who was eyeing her.

"Hi, do you mind if I sit here?" Without waiting for an answer, a young woman settled into the chair next to Natalie, introducing herself as Bettina. "Is this your first time at this event?" she asked.

"I'm Natalie. Yes, first time. I'm just visiting my cousins and celebrating my birthday tonight."

"Happy birthday! But I have to ask, why did they bring you here of all places? I'm so tired of hearing these old songs."

Natalie wasn't sure what Bettina meant about why her cousins brought her to the fete, but she offered to go and give the DJ some song requests.

"Excuse me. Excuse me," Natalie shouted above the music. She saw written in neon green across his black tee-shirt "DJ Sinatra - King of Classic Calypso & Spouge."

"Can you play something by Shontelle or HypaSounds?" she shouted above the blare of a calypsonian who was trying to find his brother.

"Who is dem?" the gray-haired DJ shouted back, pushing his old-school Koss headset back on his head.

"What?" Natalie could not believe what he asked but shrugged it off. "Look, can you at least play something from this millennium?" she asked sarcastically and stalked back to the table.

"Any luck with the DJ?" Bettina asked on Natalie's return.

"That remains to be seen, or rather heard." Natalie dryly responded. "You asked me why my cousins brought me here, but why are *you* here?"

"I bring my great-grandmother to this every year," Bettina replied, pointing to a petite silver-haired woman gliding a walker across the dance floor to *Sweet Spouge Music* by a popular seventies duo. "She doesn't get out too often."

"Your great-grandmother?"

"Oh, you really don't know? This is the annual LIBRA fete."

"What's LIBRA?"

Bettina opened her small purse, pulled out the entry ticket and handed it to Natalie. Across the gold ticket in bold black letters Natalie read, "The Long Island Bajan Retirees Association Invites...Wait! Retirees?" Natalie squealed. "I can't believe I'm spending my thirtieth birthday in New York partying with retirees. I could have stayed in Barbados and celebrated with my girls in the Gap."

High and Dry Clean

Dianne Weatherhead

"That will be $375," said the young, blonde woman behind the register, her frosty smile as chilly as the Boston air whipping outside the luxury brand store.

"Tyrell, you really spending that kinda money on a belt?" Catrina's eyes widened..

"Girl, hush nuh!" Tyrell silenced his girlfriend as he handed his lone credit card to the retail assistant who completed the transaction. "At least it on sale," he whispered.

The two braced themselves for the cold as they exited the store.

"Girl, you know I going home in a couple weeks for the first time since I left nine years ago. I ain't see de fellas since high school, and I got to look fresh. Yesterday I buy a pair of the latest Air Jordans, a Louis Vuitton cap, and a sweet looking, thick, thick, thick gold rope chain with a diamond pendant. Cheese-on-bread, I gine be sharper than sugar cane leaves." The smile on Tyrell's face could not stretch any wider, and Catrina noticed the obvious pep in his step. He was definitely feeling himself.

"Why you feel you got to impress people, doh?" Catrina asked. "Just go home and enjoy yuhself and be yuhself."

"You know some Bajans feel once you live in America money as easy to come by as do-rei-me. I just want to look like I make something of myself."

"Tyrell, you work hard and support yourself making decent money," Catrina said, trying to reassure him. "Your friends in Barbados don't do no better or worse than you. Everybody just trying to make ends meet. So you worrying about what people are going to think and then coming back to a credit card bill you can't even afford to pay off? That make sense to you?"

"Ahhh, that is where you wrong." Tyrell's sly smile hinted at a devilish scheme as they stopped at a pizzeria for lunch. "When I get back I gine return most of the things to the stores and get the money refunded. I don't plan on wearing all the expensive designer clothes. I gine jes hang dem up so my family could see the labels." Tyrell tapped his temple with a gloved finger. "See, I am a thinking man."

Catrina rolled her eyes and shook her head.

"Boss man! Welcome home!" Tyrell's friends greeted him at a popular sports bar perched on a rocky outcropping above rolling waves, where about six of them had arranged to meet. The salt-laden air mixed with the aroma of flying fish nuggets, breadfruit chips, and fried coconut shrimp at a nearby table made Tyrell's stomach rumble. He swaggered over to the large booth, his leather cap, with the recognizable designer LV motif, slightly twisted to the side, and the front of his white, over-priced Armani tee-shirt tucked into his trendy distressed jeans, making sure to reveal the iconic Gucci double G buckle.

Fist bumps and back-slapping half hugs were doled out as Tyrell's buddies shared in the excitement of having him back on the island after his extended absence.

"Leh we get some drinks to start the evening off right," suggested one of the young men, beckoning a server over to take their orders.

"So Rell, you look like America treating you real good," commented Damian.

"Man, I can't complain," Tyrell replied, nonchalantly shrugging his shoulders and slowly removing his Prada sunglasses to hang them on the rapper-style gold chain.

Just then, a shadow stretched across the table. It was Javon, Tyrell's cousin.

"Hail, Tyrell. Fellas." Javon curtly acknowledged the group with a nod, and sat without waiting for an invitation.

"Javon, wha you doing here?" Tyrell asked, his face tightening.

"I stopped by the house and Aunt Glenda say you was here with some of your boys, so I come to see my long-lost cousin," he sneered.

There was no love lost between the two young men. Growing up, Javon constantly bullied Tyrell, and when the latter moved to the US his cousin was obviously jealous.

The server returned with an assortment of beer, rum and Coke, soft drinks and fruity concoctions. The friends toasted Tyrell's success and clinked their glasses.

Oblivious to the tension, one of the guys they called Micey, asked, "So what you do up there?"

"I work for a construction company," replied Tyrell, sipping his ice-cold lime squash.

"You must be one of the top dogs at the company," said Micey.

"Is that right?" asked Javon, snickering.

"I wouldn't say I'm one of the top dogs, but I'm doing okay." Tyrell averted his eyes.

"Just okay? Looking at all the name brands you wearing from head to toe, you doing better than okay, man," said Antoine. "The next trip here you gine be flying in on your own private jet." The other men nodded in agreement.

"We glad for you, man," Antoine added. "It's good when you can climb your way to the top of the corporate ladder."

Javon burst out laughing, slapping the table, causing some of the drinks to spill.

Trying to catch his breath, he sputtered, "Climb to the top! That is a good one!" Another spurt of laughter erupted from deep in his chest.

"Wha he laughing suh hard at?" Micey asked.

"Javon, I think you should leave, just guhlong wherever it is you got to go" Tyrell said, trying to quell his rising anger.

"I think you right, Cuz," Javon said, rising from the booth seat. "But wha wunna need to know," he continued, pausing dramatically and lowering his voice, "is that Tyrell really climb to the top of the ladder, cause he is jes a roofer." Javon's chortling faded as he left the restaurant.

The group sat in stunned silence.

Fuming and embarrassed, Tyrell excused himself and left. Catrina's words rang in his head: "Just enjoy yourself and be yourself." *Too late for that now.* After a solitary walk along the beach, he headed back to his mother's house. *This night certainly can't get any worse*, he thought.

"Rell, that is you?" his mother called from her bedroom when she heard the side door open and close.

"Yes, Ma."

Tyrell headed to his bedroom but stopped abruptly in the doorway. The blue chenille bedspread covering the twin bed was sprinkled with small pieces of paper. He picked up one after the other wondering where they had come from. It took him only a few seconds to realize they were clothing tags. His mother entered the room with an armful of freshly laundered and folded clothes.

"Rell, I see you had nuff new clothes hang up. But why you dint tek off de tags, doh? And yuh know yuh got to wash new clothes before yuh could wear dem, cause yuh doan know who put dem on before you. So I wash all of dem fuh you. And I doan know how you does dry clean something. Whoever hear bout dry water?"

Tyrell fell across the bed howling like a wounded dog, "No, man, noooooo!"

Supersized Supermodel

Suzanne Durant

Apart from a few loyal followers, no one at secondary school liked Michelle Teller. She was a pretty girl, but her beauty was only surface level. She bullied people and constantly bragged about how her mother who lived in California was soon sending for her, and once there, she planned to become a big-time model and actress. Soon after graduating from fifth form, Michelle was on a plane to Los Angeles, California.

"Mummy, you could enroll me in modeling school?" were the first words out of her mouth as soon as her mother picked her up from the airport.

"Well hello to you too. And what modeling school? I putting you in high school and when you graduate, then we will talk about modeling school," her mother, Claudette, informed her.

"But Mummy..." Michelle began and quickly stopped when her mother glared at her.

At high school, Michelle soon became close friends with a clique who had a reputation as bullies and snobs. She had the perfect personality and the look to fit in. She spoke with an affected American accent, wore elaborate hairstyles, adorned her eyes with thick sweeping eyelashes, wore the trendiest clothes and gleefully picked on and tormented others at the school.

During her two years of high school, she constantly took selfies with her new friends and posted them to her social media. The photos suggested she was living an extravagant life. One was of her at the beach posing provocatively in a string bikini with the caption, "Rihanna ain't got nothing on me." Michelle's clique of friends were from wealthy families and a couple of them were the children of actors. When she visited the home of one whose father was an actor, she took a selfie posing in front of their home leaning on a white Ferrari parked in front of a three-garage mansion. She posted that one on social media with the caption, "Home sweet home. Life in LA is great."

"They don't like me in Barbados, well too bad," she said while posting one of her many selfies. "They going see how I living like a celebrity over here. America is going to make me a supermodel and a super actress. I could never be that in little, dinky Barbados."

Just as she did at school in Barbados, Michelle put the bare minimum of effort into her studies, confident that she would soon be a super star. Michelle was a bright girl, but she saw no use for school work, not when she believed she could easily get where she wanted to go with her looks and a dazzling personality she could turn on like a switch.

Once she completed high school, Michelle accosted her mother again about modeling school.

"You need to be thinking about college first," Claudette said. "Work for a year and then go to college. While at college maybe you could do modeling school on the side."

"Yeah, but you said we could look at modeling once I finished school."

"I know what I said, but Shelly you have to understand how hard it is out there. You may not get your dream job right away. Get a degree in case modeling does not come through."

"Mummy, I hear you, but I going after my dream of modeling."

At first, Claudette was going to protest. She loved her daughter and wanted the best for her, but she knew how tough it was for Caribbean immigrants with no skills or poor qualifications in America. Claudette had immigrated to the US in her thirties and attended college during the day while working at a cleaning company every night. After college, she had gotten a job first, as an office clerk at a real estate company before being promoted to office administrator. Once she had enough money saved, she had been able to bring her daughter to join her, so she too could benefit from the academic and career opportunities that abounded in the US. She was disappointed that Michelle had not made a proper effort with her studies in Barbados and when she saw the average grades from high school and the bogus posts on her social media, she knew her daughter had to learn about life the hard way.

"Ok, let's do this," she said one day. "You go ahead and look for this modeling job. But I am not paying to send you to any modeling school. If you can get that done, I will support you."

Michelle clapped her hands and hugged her mother, promising she would soon be strutting her stuff down runways in the US and Europe. Claudette returned the hug and patted her patronizingly on her back.

After getting the names of modeling agencies from her cohort of ex-school friends, Michelle eagerly hit the streets of Los Angeles to show her mother, and Barbados, that she was on her way. She posted a video of herself swaggering into a modeling agency and waiting in the reception area for an appointment she had been able to set up.

"I got this," she said, nodding into the camera and giving the deuces hand gesture just before being called in for an interview. But with no modeling experience, the agency gently rejected her.

The rejections continued over the course of two months and Michelle became despondent. But Claudette had no sympathy for her. After two days of seeing Michelle curled up at home watching television, Claudette yanked the blanket off of her one morning.

"If you tink you gine lie round my house doing nothing but watching TV, you must be crazy. Get yuh behind up off my couch and continue searching for this modeling thing you so hot for, or get a job. And you need to start looking at colleges too."

"Can I work at your company, Mummy? I don't know where to look for a job," Michelle whined.

"Find your own job. Now get up and get moving. Don't let me come back home and find out you been here the whole day."

Michelle pouted as her mother left the house and reluctantly went and took a shower to start her day. Climbing into an Uber she had called, she made her way to downtown Los Angeles to see what she could find. She went to several retail stores, but no one was hiring.

"I know one place that is looking for people," a young retail assistant offered after she overheard Michelle being let down by the floor manager.

"Really?" Michelle's face brightened. "Where?" As she looked at the girl, she thought she looked familiar.

"Around the corner. FastBurger is looking for people."

"A fast-food place? You mussee mad!" Michelle's Bajan accent came out in full force. She could not believe that this lowly salesgirl was recommending a fast-food joint to someone of her caliber.

"Just a suggestion, especially if you're desperate for a job."

Michelle cut her eye, stupsed, and walked away. The girl watched Michelle leave and then collapsed into laughter.

"Gloria, what's up with you?" her colleague, who was hanging dresses on a clothes rack, asked.

"Did you see that girl I was talking to?"

The girl nodded.

"I went to school with her in Barbados. She either did not recognize me, or she pretended she did not recognize me. She was such a pain at school, and it looks like she still is. She now lives here in California and keeps giving people the impression on social media that she is leading this fabulous, glamorous life. She also brags about how she is going to be this big-time model."

"Well, she looks pretty enough to be one."

"She only looks that way on the outside. She is a bully and a snob. The whole of Barbados will soon know about her, but not in the way she expects," she said with a devilish smirk.

After a week-long search for a job, Michelle came up empty. When she had not been successful at retail, she tried searching for bank and general office jobs but she was not qualified enough for them. Claudette offered to call the cleaning company she had worked at while in college, but after Michelle got over her shock, she outright refused.

"Who me? Cleaning? Oh please! How degrading." Michelle had a sour expression on her face. "I wouldn't be caught dead doing that kind of work *or* working at a fast-food place. What would my two thousand followers on social media think?"

During another week of no success with her job search, Michelle was passing FastBurger when she saw the "Hiring" sign in the window. She mentally wrestled with herself for a couple minutes before reluctantly entering the restaurant. It was clean and smelled nice, and at 10:00 a.m. it was not too busy. Plus, the staff looked smart in their black and gold uniforms.

Two weeks into her job at FastBurger, Michelle was slowly overcoming her discomfort with her new position in life. She still posted pictures of herself but never in her work uniform, and never around the restaurant. She maintained the image of someone who was excelling in life and on her way to becoming a model.

One day, she was working the drive-thru window when she heard someone at the ordering area, which was just across from her, squeal in a distinctly Bajan accent, "Wait, Michelle Teller? Dah is you?"

Looking around, she saw three girls at the counter, one of whom was the girl from the retail store who had told her about FastBurger. Suddenly, she realized who the girl was: Glorey Jones, who she had bullied at school in Barbados. In fact, the other two girls she recognised as Sharon Hallway and Vikki Belle who had also been victims of her bullying back then.

"Yuh looking good super modeling yuh outfit behind that register, girl," Sharon taunted.

"Yuh want fries with that shake?" Vikki said, trying to stifle a giggle but failing.

"Supersize my burger, yuh hear supermodel," Glorey said and then roared with laughter.

The three girls couldn't help their raucous laughter as they left after receiving their orders. Michelle, meanwhile, was mortified and felt like sinking into the floor. That feeling intensified when she got home and checked her phone. Posted on social media was an unflattering picture of her at work: her usually well made-up face was oily, and her uniform had a few food stains. Under the photo was the caption, "Michelle Teller is modeling a lovely outfit from FastBurger, a popular fast-food restaurant in Los Angeles. Her preferred mode of transportation is the bus, and the house she claimed is hers is a lie - big, fat, and juicy like the burgers she serves at the drive-thru window. Michelle Teller, you ain't no supermodel, you are a super liar."

When Claudette came home, she listened patiently as her daughter, through tears, told her what happened. She rubbed her daughter's back, telling her everything would be all right.

That is what you get, Claudette thought with a smile easing onto her face, *when you try to make people think yuh living a "superlife." Good job, Glorey.*

Glossary

Some of you, especially those who are not Barbadian (or Bajan as we are commonly called) may not be familiar with some of the words and expressions the characters in the stories used. To help you better understand and appreciate these terms, we have provided a glossary.

Bakes are fried dough snacks.

Bread-and-two is a salt bread (a bun) with two fish cakes stuffed inside it.

Breadfruit is a large, round, starchy fruit of a tropical tree.

Broke her pooch is an expression used to show that a person has hurt their butt.

Catspraddle means to fall with limbs splayed.

Cheese on bread is an exclamation expressing surprise, anger, enjoyment, etc.

Cou-cou and saltfish is a traditional and popular cornmeal (polenta) and okra dish usually served with codfish and lots of gravy. Flying fish is also a very popular complement to the cou-cou.

Cuh-dear is used to express sympathy to someone; it is the same as saying "poor thing".

Cut her eye/cut eye is the rolling, squinting and sharp blinking of the eyes with a look of disgust/disdain/scorn on the face (stink eye). Can be accompanied by stupsing, smacking (sounds made with the mouth), neck rolling, and/or other body gestures that show extreme displeasure. The receiver of a cut eye can feel insulted.

Dunks are small round tropical fruit with a large dimply seed. They have a yellow to orange-brown color when ripe.

Don't fool yuh foot is an expression meaning "do not pretend you do not know".

Home training is often used to reference that you do not have any proper upbringing. This means that you were not taught how to behave well/appropriately especially if you are out in public.

Lead pipes are baked goods that are hard, dense, elongated pastries shaped like a pipe.

Lime (as in 'to lime') means to hangout; be idle.

Mauby is a bittersweet brew made with the bark of the Snakewood (Colubrina elliptica) tree. It is an acquired taste, but is quite refreshing when consumed ice cold.

Mobbaton means a big or a large amount of something. Bajans may also use this to refer to a particular part of the body.

Pooch does not mean a dog; it is used to reference a person's butt.

Poppit means an idiot. You do not want a Bajan calling you this.

Redcaps are airport porters. On arrival to the airport from travel, they assist with your luggage and are easily identified by their red caps.

Stupse appears quite often in the short stories. This is when someone sucks their teeth in annoyance or disgust. If you are not sure what that sounds like, ask a Bajan. They will most likely oblige you with a demonstration.

The Gap is St. Lawrence Gap, which is a popular south coast (Christ Church) entertainment area.

Turnovers are sticky, baked buns stuffed with sweetened grated coconut.

Wuhloss is an exclamation to express surprise or excitement at something overwhelming or unexpected.

Young yam is used to refer to an older person, usually female, perceived as acting younger than their age.

Acknowledgements

This book was definitely a labor of love for the two of us and we enjoyed creating the characters, the plots and the scenes. As we plugged away at our computers every chance we got to complete this trove of Bajan treasures, we had a lot of support along the way.

First we want to thank our dear friend and fellow member of our WhatsApp Cawmere 6th Form chat group, Betty Bayley. Your contribution and support during the embryonic stage of this project was much appreciated.

We also extend a big thank you to our proofreaders, **Valerie Anderson** and **Paullee Weatherhead**. We read and reread our stories, but thanks to your eagle-eyed diligence, you caught some things we missed. We appreciate all you did to help us put out a book that we can be proud of.

Thank you so much **Eden Weekes** for the wonderful job you did creating our book cover. It took some time, but we got there. We appreciate your patience and your speed in getting the cover done as quickly as we needed it. You are truly talented. Keep up the good work.

Many times, we would find ourselves glued to our computers engrossed in getting our story ideas down. Unfortunately for our families, those were our "Do Not Disturb" times. However, we cannot thank our families enough for their support and encouragement. It would be remiss of us not to include your names: **Victor**, **Jonathan**, and **Samara** (Suzanne's family) and **Gary**, **Troy**, and **Janae** (Dianne's family).

Finally, we thank all you readers because without you, there would be no book.

Afterword

From Suzanne

After publishing a few novels, I wanted to write a collection of Bajan short stories that were fun to read. Stories that showed people in various situations with unexpected results designed to draw a laugh out of my readers. I did this with **Where There's A Will** (2022).

The response to the book was so good that I decided to create another Bajan short story collection, but this time as a collaboration with another Bajan who, at the time, could not see how talented a writer she is. That writer is Dianne Weatherhead.

I approached her about the project and she readily agreed. Initially, nerves made her hesitant, but I could see that she really wanted to do this. After many meetings and much collaboration, **A Taste of Home** was born.

We are both so very proud of the work we have done on this collection, and I am particularly proud that after dipping her toes into the world of writing, Dianne is now ready to jump in, so expect more work from her.

Because we are both Barbadian-born and have adopted America as home, we decided to write stories showing the Bajan/American experience. Just like my solo collection, the stories are lighthearted and intended to make you laugh as we see Bajans caught up in various funny situations, Bajans speaking their language, and Bajans highlighting their snacks and delicacies like Tea Times, mauby, sweetbread, and cou-cou and flying fish.

We did it, Dianne! We did it, dear readers! I hope you enjoyed reading the stories as much as we enjoyed creating them for you.

From Dianne

A dream deferred is finally a reality. I wanted to write a book for many years but was daunted by the thought of tackling a novel.

When Suzanne published her first book, she encouraged me to do the same, and she relentlessly continued to do so. After the release of her collection of short stories, **Where There's A Will** (2022), she again tried to persuade me, and again I hesitated, so she invited me to co-author with her. It felt like easing into the shallow end of the pool instead of diving into the deep end.

It was fun and challenging creating the characters and scenarios in this short story collection. I hope readers enjoyed the lighthearted entertainment and maybe saw a familiar persona or situation.

I have learned so much from Suzanne about the writing and self-publication processes, and I will definitely be playing catch-up. I'm now eager to dust off the other stories that I had stashed away on my mental bookshelf and share them with my fellow Bajans and the world.

One More Thing

We invite you to email us at **diandsuz@gmail.com** with your comments about the stories. We also welcome reviews of this short story collection on Amazon, and we invite you to follow us on Amazon. Please let others know what you thought about **A Taste of Home**.

The email address is **edenartemail@gmail.com** for those of you interested in having your book cover done by the very talented **Eden Weekes**.

We could not end without saying thank you so much for purchasing and reading **A Taste of Home**. Cheers.

About the Authors

Suzanne Durant

Reading and writing from the time she could string sentences together and hold a pencil, Suzanne Durant has authored and self-published four fiction books and one nonfiction book to date: **Her Own Daughter** (2010), **Dark Energy** (2014), **Perfect Nightmare** (2016), **Where There's a Will and Other Short Stories** (2022), and **Ladies, Let's Get Real About You Life and Love** (2022).

Before relocating from Barbados to the United States, Suzanne was an English tutor for sixteen years at Barbados's University of the West Indies. Now, she is focused on her first love: crafting fiction and nonfiction. She also ghostwrites autobiographies and memoirs, she edits and proofreads fiction and nonfiction, and she provides writing and grammar assistance to beginner authors.

In her free time Suzanne is reading or watching movies and enjoying whatever time she can with family and friends. Once she is home in Barbados, she and the beach are best friends.

Dianne Weatherhead

Dianne Weatherhead has lived in the United States for over thirty-five years, but her Barbadian roots still run deep. She holds a degree in Broadcast Journalism from Brooklyn College, NY.

After working briefly in television news, she discovered she enjoyed a more creative form of writing. When she opted to leave the traditional workforce to raise her family, she became a freelance writer. Her writings have ranged from newsletters for non-profit organizations to scripts for business features, oratorical presentations to poetry, and gospel tracts to resumes.

When she's not writing, her other creative outlets include beaded jewelry making, sewing and crafting. Glass-blowing and silversmithing are next on her list. *A Taste of Home and Other Short Stories* is her first published work of fiction. She is currently working on her first novel.

Made in the USA
Middletown, DE
11 June 2024